George Scithers's

Con-Committee
Chairman's Guide

George Scithers's

Con-Committee
Chairman's Guide

By George H. Scithers, F.M & Elinor Busby, Howard Devore, Earl Kemp, Bob Pavlat, & Bill Evans

edited and originally published by Dick Eney
[whose remarks appear in square brackets]
Operation Crifanac CCLXXVII

It's Eney's Fault

Dedicated to:
The New York and Philadelphia branches of the ISA

I bet you'd do it all over again if you got the chance,
you impentinent faaaaans!

TABLE OF CONTENTS

ARTWORK

Jim Cawthorn: Cover, 21, 23
Roy G. Krenkel: 13, 25
George Barr: 17
George H. Scithers: 22
Dom Orejudos: 29

"Begin at the beginning, and go on till
you come to the end: then stop."
— *The King of Hearts*

0.0 PREFACE TO THE THIRD EDITION

Since the first edition was published, World Science Fiction Conventions have increased in size ten-fold and more. (So have prices.) This, then, is a guide to putting on an ordinary convention focusing on science fiction, fantasy, or both with an attendance of around 400 to 600 people and a single track of program items. Many of the basic principles still apply to conventions of any size.

0.1 FOREWORD

This, then, is a guide to how to put on a World Science Fiction Convention. Not necessarily *any* World Science Fiction Convention, but at least it'll tell you how we think we should have (and in some cases did) put on the 21st World Science Fiction Convention back on Labor Day weekend, 1963.

There are three basic ideas we'd like to get across:
1. Putting on a con isn't as dreadful as it's said to be;
2. Though you certainly can't and won't please everyone, you should pick who you want to antagonize and then do it firmly; and,
3. Finally, don't work yourself to death if you do put on a con — it isn't necessary to do so.

0.2 GETTING THE BID

This is a subject that we're not really qualified to talk about, since we made an uncontested bid. But don't think for a moment that we're going to let *that* stop us; we can give advice on this subject as readily as on those for which our ignorance isn't quite so abysmal.

To begin with, it's necessary to show people that you

are serious; that you *do* want to put on the Umptyth World Science Fiction Convention. And to do *that,* you (the prospective con committee) have got to take stock of yourselves and decide if you do, indeed, want to take all the responsibility and the work this entails.

To decide this, you'll have to take a long hard look at a couple of local factors. How's the local hotel situation? What sort of deal will the local places offer? Basically, you must have a tentative reservation with a satisfactory hotel before you can go any further in putting on a con.

Mind you, don't *unnecessarily* close the deal before you have the bid — especially if the hotel is holding out for $$$ for convention facilities. Seacon found the hotels more anxious to meet their needs *after* they had the bid, and did not actually name the site until around New Year's 1962.

Of course, you must do your scouting and dickering during your bidding year. If you can have your site chosen and terms sealed when you make the bid, all the better; but all you need is a deal that you *can* take if you can't better it.

The requirements? Well, does your hotel have the characteristics that you admired in previous con hotels? No, that's not where you start. The first question is, "Does the hotel have a big enough meeting room?" The second: "Does the hotel have enough rooms available to hold the attendees?" The answers to these two questions will quickly narrow down the selection of hotels in your city to a reasonable few.

(If you've never had to ask such questions before, the secret — supposing that you don't have unlimited time and telephone privileges available — is to get hold of a recent issue of *The Hotel Redbook,* which lists such data for every hotel in the country that's big enough to hold any kind of convention. Your local Chamber of Commerce can probably let you see their copy.)

Then look into other problems. Is the room rate offered to the con reasonable? Are the meeting rooms laid out effectively? How are the hotel dining facilities? [In DC we determined this by Moffatt's Test, in the restaurants. Order a salad with Roquefort dressing; if it's non-synthetic dressing, with real cheese in lumps, the place passes. Bars are tested by Rotsler's Test; their daiquiris should be cold, and taste neither too harsh (= too much rum) nor too sour (= too much lime). Chinese restaurants may be roughly appraised by Evans' Test; the smaller the proportion of "Western" dishes on the menu, the higher the score.] And — does the management want to have you?

The other local factor: who do you have locally (near enough to hit if they goof up) to put on the con? Now, this is a highly variable number. We functioned with four principal committee members, plus about six highly valuable (and willing, and competent) hose carriers, plus about a dozen and a half local and distant fans who gave us a hand. Some committees have been larger; some folk have put on cons with even fewer principals. All we can say is that we apparently had enough and not too many. Too few principals means too much work for each; I suppose too many principals would lead to fights, but that's just theorizing, since we didn't have any.

The essential point is this. At various times before and especially during the con, the committee have to be at n different places at one time. If n exceeds the number of people available, willing, and competent to do whatever's come up, you're in trouble. If not, you've got things well under control.

Other matters: get a fixed room price from the prospective hotel; you'll need it for arguing your bid. Get a banquet price, as firm a one as you can this early . . . maybe two prices, allowing a choice of entrees.

And Pick a Guest of Honor. This is a bit of delicate manoeuvring. The identity of the GoH is traditionally kept secret until after you've definitely been selected as the next con site. Hence, your inquiries have to be on the basis of, *"If* we get the next con, will you . . . ?" It might even be a good idea to pick out an emergency alternate Guest of Honor, just in case. On secrecy we had no trouble, even though a goodly number of the Washington Science Fiction Association, the local club, knew who he was.

A special problem may come up. What if one of you and your competitors pick the same GoH? The simple solution to that one, if you're worried, is to tell the chairman of the con immediately before your own what you're worried about, tell him who your choice is, and ask *him* what to do. Clearly, you can trust his impartiality; it's one of the characteristics of the job.

Beyond that? Throw a party at a couple of cons previous to the one you're bidding for. See that you get enough plugs in the fanzines for people to know you're bidding. Throw a bash at the Midwestcon. And don't knock yourselves out *getting* the bid; there's lots of work to come, and you need a functioning committee to do it.

0.3 MONEY

Before you actually win your bid, that's your problem. Entertainment expenses, printing, and publicity are all things that the prospective con committee will have to cover, for the time being, out of their own pockets.

After you've been selected — well, if you watch out for expenses and (as Busby once put it) hit anyone who suggests you spend money on anything not absolutely essential, then the advance registration (the memberships you sell at the con just previous to your own) will be adequate for your immediate financial needs. (We'd better be quite clear here that this is essentially a discussion of U.S. conditions and U.S. cons. Those overseas will meet different situations about which Americans know almost nothing.) You can also hope for, but of course are not guaranteed, about $300, which you are expected to pass on to the next con from your profits. [No more than $300 is needed; more than this would be undesirable, aside from the overseas exchange problems that might arise.] It represents valuable working capital, as well as being insurance in case things turn out less profitably than you had expected. In previous years, cons have traditionally sweated out bankruptcy in addition to their other worries. In previous years, too, cons have traditionally depended on the auction to balance the books. Well, auctions are no longer what they once were. On the other hand, the $3 membership fee has pretty well insured that a reasonably well-run convention won't go broke.

(In passing: some folk have cried that the last three cons have done so well, financially, that we don't need the $3 fee. This is nonsense. None of the last three con committees would have felt secure, for the duration of their cons, that they'd stay out of the poorhouse; none of the last three con committees would have gotten *any* enjoyment out of their own cons; the publication of the *Proceedings* could not have been contemplated; and, finally, *our* con committee would not have bid under the $2 membership fee. If some group wants to try to put on a con for $2, they can try; the present Society rules do not set the membership fees at all — but none of *us* would care to have anything to do with such an attempt.)

The $3 *doesn't* insure that you can't go broke if you try, though. The way to make certain that you don't try is to run an accounting of all expenses, incurred and estimated, assuming everything will cost a bit more than you hope. Next, compare that with an estimate of all income, received and anticipated, assuming that you'll get somewhat *less* than you're sure of (for example, don't assume *any* income from the auction at all). As long as income exceeds outgo, you're safe — but keep checking, particularly before each decision to spend money on anything new.

Final note on preregistration and money: we made our bookkeeping easier by using a two-part registration card. One half of this was the membership card itself, the other was our record of the name and address of the member. The membership-card portion (which had to be signed by a member of our committee to be valid) also served as the receipt for the membership fee. Both halves carried a pre-printed serial number; both were tagged according to whether the member had paid $2 or $3. (3) [In explanation: the fees for the Discon were $2 for membership in the con (or $1 for overseas fans) and $1 more for actual attendance. The entire $3 could be paid in advance; or $2 could be paid beforehand and $1 at the con.

Of course, somebody who hadn't registered beforehand could pay the entire $3 on arrival. With this sort of thing to keep straight, the multi-purpose card was well worth the cost of preparing it.]

And a concluding note: there is always a demand for low membership numbers. To meet this demand, we numbered ours from zero to 900 (though we didn't have that many registrations); to -30, to i30 (that is, to 30 times the square root of minus one, a type of numbering used by mathematicians) and to -i30. The Guest of Honor, of course, got card number (+) 1 and his wife, number 2.

0.4 PROGRESS REPORTS & THE PROGRAM BOOK

The best advice we can give on these: don't kill yourselves putting such things out. (We damn near did.) Some people — in fact, what is important, some members of past con committees — think that the quality of the progress reports and of the program booklet is most important, since it is this quality that the non-attending members have to appreciate, and which keeps them sending in their $2s. Ours, three-color covers and all, got little reaction; but, on the other hand, a particularly bad set of progress reports would probably arouse considerable resentment.

A good number of potential advertisers expect a certain degree of quality reproduction. A book publisher, for instance, might like to place an ad for one of his new titles. He could hardly be expected to appreciate a mimeographed reproduction of his ad, however well done. Also, no single year's run of progress reports are actually a separate entity unto themselves. Conventions, for better or worse, are part of a very big continuing whole. Anything one convention does reflects on the following conventions. Advertisers look at the overall quality of the progress reports, as well as the convention program books, in making the decision to place ads. If your committee allows the quality to slip below a certain normal, *you* mightn't feel its effects; they may, however, come re-

soundingly home a year or so later, much to the dismay of the then-current committee.

One of the best ways to avoid killing yourselves on the program book would be to set a relatively early deadline for the ads, and then *stick to it*. Since we had our own printing facilities we let things slip in up to about two weeks before the con itself. But the extra money just wasn't worth the consequent flurry and flap of finishing printing, and assembling all of the program book at the very last minute. It is generally worth while to hold up on the program schedule until quite late, since there are inevitably last minute additions and deletions in the schedule. Since, in many printing arrangements, the center two or four sheets can be the last printed and assembled, the schedule of the program is usually in the center pages of the program book. (But be sure *your* printer does things this way if you go commercial.)

Our program book was done on a local machine, the Chairman's Ancient and Venerable Multilith, and assembly and folding were done free with the assistance of the local club. (Well, almost free; the con funds were used for Pepsis and potato chips and stuff for the assembly party.) The inescapable costs were for paper and (for Progress Reports and non-attending members' copies of the Program Book) postage. (This last is a not-inconsiderable sum.)

Ad prices? We tried an innovation; making the pro space charges and the fan space charges the same, instead of the usual "soak the pros" arrangements of the past. It may have netted us some goodwill from the prozines and book publishers; we just don't know. On the other hand, I'm sure the practice of charging more for copy involving half-tone negatives than for copy requiring only line negatives is definitely a Good Thing. Halftone work is definitely more trouble, not only in preparation of negatives and plates, but also in the printing itself. How much should the ad prices be? If you're getting your Progress Reports and Program Book run off by an outside firm, make sure your charges are greater than the cost of the extra amount the printer will charge you for that much extra page count. If you're doing your own printing, charge as much for the ads as you would if you were sending the book out to be printed. In short: make the charges fairly stiff, so that the extra work you put into the publications because of the ads is well repaid.

(Special note: almost all printers underestimate the time it'll take them to finish and deliver . . . it is sort of a tradition among printers. Set your deadline for return of Progress Reports and Program Book from the printer accordingly, and make it clear in your contract with the printer that late delivery voids the contract.)

0.5 HUGOS

Assemble the Hugos (the awards themselves) early. (This advice has been passed from con committee to con committee for years. As far as I know, no one has ever followed it. Chicon III Hugos were assembled *during* the con. With the Discon, final assembly was done just 24 hours before the awards were handed out. Hugo assembly at Seacon was Thursday afternoon immediately preceding the con, with the phone ringing about ten times per hour.)

Costs: the Hugos (plating, casting, machining and all) cost us about $90 for a set of seven. They'd have been lots more if it had not been for Howard DeVore's contacts and hard work. Bases cost about $19 for another set of seven. The plaques, which were photo-engraved, cost about $30 for the set. They were glued, not screwed, to the bases, using epoxy glue.

A note on the rocket ships themselves: our set was cast in aluminum, and then plated with copper and nickel, and finally with chromium. Although there are advantages in the aluminum (less cost, less weight) the plating difficulty outweighs those advantages. For one thing, if anything goes at all wrong with the plating, blisters, stripped places, and the like, then it's impossible to strip the plating off and start over again, since anything that will get the chromium off will attack the aluminum with vast enthusiasm. For another thing, while a pit in an aluminum casting can only be sanded out (if it isn't too deep) a pit in a brass casting can be filled with solder before the final machining. Another point: the chrome doesn't look enough better than just nickel to be worth either the extra cost or the risk of the chrome blistering or peeling. For future Hugos, we recommend either brass casting, plated with nickel only; or possibly an aluminum casting, either polished as is or anodized, but definitely *not* plated.

In addition to the Hugos, the Discon I also gave two brass plaques: one to the Guest of Honor, Will F. Jenkins, and the other to the toastmaster, Isaac Asimov. These were each about four inches across and about one inch thick, which made them very impressively heavy. The toastmaster's had "Toastmaster — Discon — 21st World Science Fiction Convention" on the face, together with the witch-flask/scientist-testtube emblem from the membership cards. Both words and illustration were photo-engraved into the metal; more precisely, into an eighth-inch-thick slab of copper which was fastened to the copper with epoxy glue. The Guest of Honor's was made the same way, with "Guest of Honor — Discon — 21st World Science Fiction Convention," and the illustration was the Owl-and-Saturn emblem from the name-card badges used at the con itself. The plaques were expensive, because photo-engraving and metal-milling are not cheap. Cost for the pair was about $40.

Now, for the voting: The rules that have been in effect since the Seacon leave the nominating procedure entirely up to the convention committee. The constitution adopted at the Discon does not change this point. Chicon III accepted nominations from anyone who wrote in. Because of worries about possible ballot-box stuffing by fictitious names, the Discon restricted nominations to people who were either members of the previous con, our own con, or both (that is, people who had paid for membership in either or both). We had no trouble with nomination-stuffing. (We understand, from confidential remarks from previous con committees, that ours was one of the few recent cons that was not troubled by ballot

DISCON
PROGRESS
REPORT

TWO

O. Barr - 1962

box stuffing attempts; Seacon was another.) On the other hand, we received only about 80 sets of nominations, which meant that the fourth and fifth positions on the list of final nominees were decided by very few votes indeed, and this is not good.

Final voting on the Hugos was limited to members of the Discon as of the date of the closing of the voting. To encourage voting, we used printed, return-addressed, postage-prepaid postcards with the names of the nominees thereon. This of course was expensive; about $16, plus printing. On the other hand, it did improve the number of votes (about 226 people voted in the final poll, not counting late votes) and it did insure against anyone not a member sending in a forged card. For future cons, I'd suggest prepaid postcards for both nominations and final votes. Be careful and proofread these final ballots; we left "Burn, Witch, Burn" off our postcard list. [If George wasn't accepting the principle of Collective Responsibility, this would read properly: "Dick Eney left `Burn, Witch, Burn' off . . ."], an omission which was very embarrassing indeed.

In calling for nominations (usually done in about your second progress report) we strongly advise printing the entire set of rules governing ballotting and eligibility; it won't eliminate all complaints about who's eligible for what, but it'll reduce the complainers to a few notorious witwants who'll complain in any event.

Another problem — but a potential one, not yet realized: what if somebody with more money than morals buys enough memberships in the con for real and/or mythical friends for this set of friends' votes may throw the nominations or the election in some or other category. Dick Lupoff raised the question a little while ago, once in a fanzine article and once in an ad for Canaveral Press, which suggested that all the ERBurroughs fans should Get Together and vote for that antique potboiler, *Savage Pellucidar*. (No, he didn't call it an antique potboiler; *I* did.) What to do? Well, we don't know. All we can say is that the con committee, by rule and by custom, has pretty wide powers to rule unsavory candidates off the ballot, and that all previous con committees will back you up if you do anything within reason.

0.6 SETTING UP THE PROGRAM

There are two basic points which must be understood before we go any further. These are the long-hidden secrets of convention-putting-on-manship. Read carefully:

1. It is better to under-program than overprogram.
2. Planning and setting up a convention can easily be done on a rainy afternoon and evening.

To the first point: it is inherent in the nature of conventions, professional authors, and fans that there are far more speakers and subjects available for presentation than there is time, at *any* convention, to present. Some of these items can be very good indeed. Some of them, almost for sure, will pop up at the last minute — a discussion of a new scientific development; the appearance of a notable author from abroad who hadn't expected to be here; a short but intensely interesting movie — any of these things will consume time on the program. Furthermore, there is a tendency for things to take longer than they are supposed to. A particularly interesting question session at the end of a controversial panel can easily, and unexpectedly, go on for an hour overtime. Auctions always try to go on for longer than they are supposed to. Movies inevitably take extra time for set-up and take-down.
Therefore: *Don't over-program.*

People who go to conventions do not like to get up at unearthly hours (like 10 or 11 AM). If you stuff too much into the program, the schedule will overflow into these hours. Again: people don't like to sit far into the night listening to lectures and panels. If you stuff too much into the program, they'll have to, to see the whole show.
Do not overprogram.

One way to arrange the program is to schedule, say, two regular program items, and follow that with an intermission; then two program items and another intermission; and so on. The intermissions will be items of flexible length and of (generally) less than maximum interest. An auction, allowing more than enough time for set-up and take-down, makes a good change of pace. It also allows the non-buyers to get out, maybe get a bite to eat, and so on. Also, a flexible-length item is a necessity every so often in order to get things back onto schedule, either by giving time to things which have run over or, very rarely, taking up slack from something that has run short. Presentation or introduction of notables is such a flexible item, *if* and only if it is run by the committee. The business meeting and presentation of minor awards are not. They vary in length all right, but the con committee has little control over how long they'll last.

Instead, the business meeting has to be buffered by some variable-length item, so that an over-or under-run won't throw remaining items off. One of the most satisfactory solutions to that is to put something which might go on and on and *on* at the end of the program for an evening, as was the case with the famous fan panel at the Detention.

But, throughout all this, you'll have to have time for these buffer items, these intermissions. And you'll only have that available time if you *don't over-program.*

And what if a program item falls through at the last minute? Or a panel doesn't materialize? What will you do with the blank time? Believe us, this is not a problem to worry about. For one thing, science fiction writers are, by and large, people with something interesting to say. If one planned speech falls through, you can (if you ask nicely) get someone from the audience — writer, editor, fan publisher — to speak on short notice. More likely, between the time the program finally goes to press and the time you learn that so-and-so has come down with an acute case of fallen armpits and can't leave home, you'll have two offers of short speeches to fill that suddenly open time. In fact, the next time *I* put on a convention, I

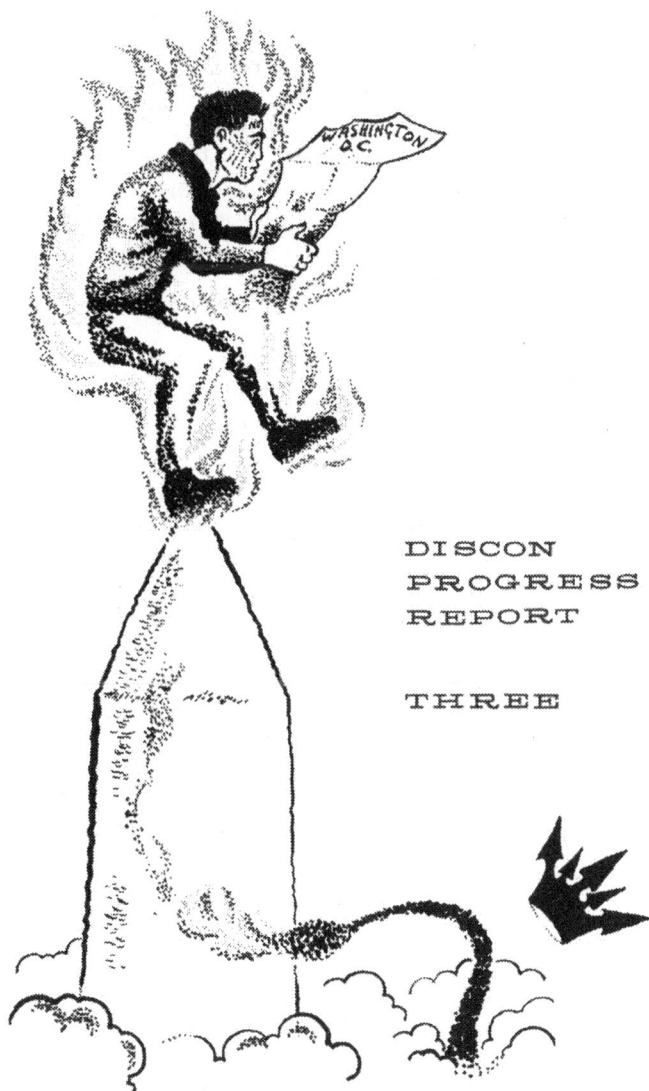

DISCON
PROGRESS
REPORT

THREE

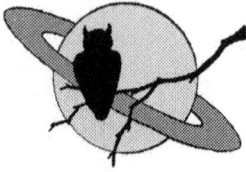

am going to list at least one half hour spot on the program as "Surprise item: to be announced." The item may be a surprise to me too, but I'm sure something will come up.

In sum, then, you do not need to over-program to make up for unexpected attrition of the speakers, you *do* need buffer time during the con to make up for things that run overtime, and there'll be excellent opportunities to put on unexpected items of interest. Therefore, do *not* put too many items into the program.

Now, the rainy afternoon and evening.

In spite of the noisy "fannish" types that boast of how little of the program they see, and suggestions that one have no program, just parties, at a con, the program *is* important. Some folk *don't* care for the program. They can stay away from the sessions, and just party or whatever. For most of the fans, younger semi-fans, the readers, and most of the pros the program is the biggest single attraction of a science fiction convention. It is for all these folk that the program is important. (But still, don't overprogram!)

It is nice to have some sort of unifying theme for the program of a con — indeed, for the whole of the con. For Chicon III, it was "Homecoming" — the grand summation of what we'd been doing for lo, these many years. For the Discon, we had several themes planned at one time or another. At one time, we planned to stress the woman's place in Science Fiction; as writer, reader, and fan. We got no further than to set up the Panel of Wives. Later, we thought of the theme of "21st Con — SF Comes of Age." We dropped *that* idea almost instantly. Next came the idea of "Illustrations and Words — The Visual Aspect of Science Fiction." There was a good bit of this in the final program; the Silverberg-Emsh-Leiber discussion of the hazards of writing a story to fit an illustration was one result of this. The panel "What Should a BEM Look Like?"

was another; the fan panel of The Art of Putting Illos on Stencils, the costume ball, and the work that went into setting it up for maximum visibility of the masqueraders, and the large space obtained for Project Art Show; Dick Lupoff's and Larry Ivie's lectures, with slides, on SF Art and The Comics — all these were aspects of the Illustration and Words theme. If we'd asked the remaining panels and speakers to make passing reference to illustration — to visualization — even if their subjects had nothing further to do with that subject, then we'd have tied that theme solidly into the program.

There is a danger in making too much of a unifying theme: people will quickly tire of too much on one topic. It is this reason, more than any other, that kept us from pushing the Illustrations and Words theme more than we did. The string of Progress Reports and the Program Book, the membership card, and the attendees' name cards carried a different theme, for instance: the combination of Science Fiction and Fantasy. In the progress reports, there was George Barr's illo; the genie of Fantasy, just received by a Stfnal extraterrestrial. In Roy Krenkel's illo, there was the robot of Science Fiction strolling through the Elysian Fields with a nymph of Fantasy. Jim Cawthorn's series showed, first, a Nazgul perched on the Washington Monument; then the Nazgul displaced by Gully Foyle; and then the whole crew of Sciencefictional and Fantasy characters drinking beer at the base of the monument. Domingo Orejudos's cover to *The Fan's Guide to Washington* showed a space-suited astronaut hanging for dear life to a witch-guided broom. And the membership card showed a test tube and skull-topped beermug (again an illustration by Jim Cawthorn) while the namecard combined the elements by indirection: the Halloweenish silhouette of an owl against, not the moon, but a ringed planet.

As it turned out, the con had a basic theme which was quite different from either of

these, hadn't been intended as the theme at all, and was exploited quite a bit as a theme when it developed. That theme was one of swordplay-and-sorcery. The sessions of the Burroughs Bibliophiles, the Burroughs panel, the musters of the Hyborean Legion, many of the costumes of the ball — all these echoed the swordplay-and-sorcery bit. There was a flavor of it, inevitably, in the Lupoff and Ivie talk. Katherine MacLean spoke of it; Lester del Rey disagreed with her on it. And after all, the very first session of the con started off with a sword fight and an incantation . . .

Now to the second point about setting up the program, that it's essentially the thing for a rainy afternoon and evening. Well, it should take but an hour or two to write up a prospective program and arrange the items in a suitable order — like, don't have all your panels on one day; don't have too many panels (two-man discussions are far more lively); leave time for such essentials as the business meeting, the banquet, and the ball — then just juggle a few loose ends around; and there you are. Of course, what you have at this point is by no means what you will actually put on, but it's a starting point. If you had a theme in mind, draw on it heavily for subjects for the planned talks and all. Now look over the program: any folk who have appeared in the last con, or in local cons, and to whom the con attendees might have been overexposed? Can you think of any nearby people who almost never get to cons, who almost never speak at cons, who might be persuaded to speak instead? In short, rewrite your program now so that it is distinct from the program of the last few worldcons and local 'claves.

Next: reach for the phone and call those whom you'd like to have who aren't too far away (and key folk should be called anyway, so long as they don't involve an overseas call). Remember, calls in the evening are cheaper. Remember too that an ordinary con has a total budget running into four figures; these calls you can afford, as long as you have checked to be sure you expect the con as a whole to be in the black.

DISCON
PROGRESS
REPORT   FOUR

The big advantage of a call: you find out at once who of the people you want will promise to be there. You can get ideas for substitute subjects. If you want to build a panel around a given subject and a given moderator, you can get from him, at once, his suggestions for other panellists. And, for the intended speaker, you pay him the compliment of letting him know he's important enough to warrant a phone call. It also gets around the problem of the intended speaker who doesn't answer your letter; for in such a case, you're in the difficult position of having to write him later and tell him if you don't hear right away, you will withdraw your invitation.

Then: write letters confirming the substance of the various phone calls to the folks who have accepted, along with any letters you write to those you didn't contact on the phone. The set of notes you have at this point isn't the final program yet, but it's the basic skeleton. You'll be arranging things, adding other items, dropping things that don't work out, from then until the convention is over; but the essential basis for a convention program is set at this point.

When to do this? ~~Well, you can wait until it rains~~ . . . If you set things up very early (on the order of nine months in advance) you'll run into a lot of people who haven't made up their minds if they'll come to the con yet. Your letter of call may persuade them to come, but on the other hand there's more time for something to come up and make them cancel their plans. Yet if you call too late, they will be irritated at being asked so much at the last minute; they may have other plans for the con weekend, or they may not have enough time to properly prepare a lecture.

For the Discon, we set up most of the convention program in July, which seemed early enough to us. There was one noisy chap who was insulted that we hadn't asked him earlier to give us the benefit of his vast wisdom in such matters. In point of fact, we never *did* ask his wisdom, either vast or partially so, on much of anything.

Which brings up another point connected with the

rainy afternoon. Since the business of planning a basic program *is* so simple, other folks will try it too. Some may send in their proposals. The good ideas, take; the ones that you don't like (note well: it's basically a question of what *you* like or don't like that must govern what goes into the program) reject. Some people may get very upset at getting their suggestions rejected . . . hard to imagine fans being so lacking in objectivity, but it has happened. If these touchy folk live in the same city, or, worse, are on the local fan club, they can raise all kinds of trouble for you. [That's what killed the Los Angeles bid for the 1964 con; the working committee was invaded by a local femmefan too touchy to snub, too influential to ignore, and too conscious of her own BNFship to accept a token post.] However, the basic rule is: who works, decides. Who doesn't work — and work hard — on the preparations (work type work, not idea-and-suggestion work) gets no say-so in how the con is run, no matter how big-named, loud-mouthed, or both. As pointed out earlier, putting on a con is a chance to pick out your enemies and *really* infuriate them.

If you are members of a local club you may be afflicted by back seat drivers who are loaded with useful suggestions but of course too busy to be on the Committee or do any work. (And of course there's always the ten percent who genuinely *are* too busy, not disinclined.) Therefore, the wise will be sure that the committee is set up *independent* of the club; that the committee (and not the club) is responsible for the con in title as well as in fact. If the committee is set up as an agent of the club, you *can* be in trouble all the way.

0.7 AUCTION MATERIAL

This is one of those tasks that can be run independently from much of the rest of setting up the con. If you have a reliable volunteer (and, let's face it, not an awful lot of fans are reliable) even if he lives in another city — New York, for choice — but is certain to attend the con, then you might turn the whole auction-collection problem over to him. In our case, we handled the auction collection by a visit to some of the editors in New York; some offers of specific items, made and accepted by mail; and by a couple of phone calls to other editors. Chicon III found that manuscripts sold well, so we made an effort to gather them. We took care to be selective; that is, we asked for (and got) only a small number of the total lot of black-and-white illos available from the magazines we approached. In addition, we made arrangements with a few of the professional artists for a very limited number of color paintings. These latter, by the way, are usually sold by the convention on some sort of profit-sharing arrangement.

If you are seriously in the bidding for a convention, previous committees will give you details on request as to the going rates and so forth. We don't recommend accepting more than a couple of items in the auction on a minimum-price basis, because this unreasonably complicates bookkeeping, as well as making the convention responsible for the minimum price if one of the items gets stolen. [As happened at Chicon III.] Auctioneers can be instructed to withdraw an item if the bidding does not go high enough, or to start specific items with a high bid; but such arrangements should be at the discretion of the con committee and its auctioneers, rather than firmly fixed in advance by the artist.

A few speciality items will do well at an auction, too, as variety items. The planetary system model constructed by Hal Clement sold very well indeed; so did the Gestetner which the Discon auctioned off.

Remember, the auction is no longer absolutely necessary for the con to make ends meet, but it does do a lot toward paying for extras like the *Proceedings*. You can put as much or as little effort into it as your own situation lets you afford. It is an important item in the program for many attendees, and they'll appreciate a good auction.

We were able to make up a list , which was distributed at registration, of all but the last-minute donations. It was useful, it was appreciated, but it was not essential.

A FAN'S SHORT GUIDE TO WASHINGTON

How to
Get around in D.C.

Do one like it if you can, don't if you can't, and don't worry about it.

0.8 HOTEL ARRANGEMENTS

Make sure that the hotel is using the same scheduling for main and minor meetings and meeting places that you are. If you've decided to have the banquet on the second day instead of the first day, check several times to be sure that the hotel has got the word. Find out well in advance, and then keep checking later, whether there are to be other groups moving into rooms right after the scheduled close of any of your meetings. One of the great advantages of Labor Day weekend is that it is a pretty dead weekend for most hotels; but it won't be completely dead, so find out who else is going to be there, and plan accordingly.

Hotels vary from city to city much more than they do within a city. For example, at Washington our auxiliary meeting rooms cost nothing. Chicon III, on the other hand, had to pay for their Project Art Show room, because all their free space was used up already. In Seattle, for a Horrible Example, the downtown hotels all wanted to charge for the use of the main meeting room. [Len Moffat says this happened at South Gate, too.] Therefore, the arrangements we cite are not necessarily typical for other cities, even in the U.S.A.

(Some hotels will offer the main hall free if given a guarantee on the number of room reservations by the con. Go slow, and get plenty of information from past committees, before agreeing to any such arrangement, because this is what cost South Gate big money — the guarantee didn't materialize.)

In D.C., we got the use of the two big meeting rooms for our scheduled meetings (that is, when we weren't officially meeting, the hotel could [and did] let those rooms out to other groups); a big display room and a connecting small meeting room throughout the duration of the con (plus the preceding day for set-up and the following day for take-down); a large suite; and two double rooms.

In return, we only had to designate the hotel (the Statler-Hilton, in Washington) as the official hotel; to distribute reservation cards with the progress reports; and to give the hotel our reasonable guess that we'd have about 300 folk from the con staying at the hotel. The hotel also gave us a flat cut-rate on rooms and suites below the normal rates; this cut-rate was offered to anyone who sent in reservations early. Concessions such as these are a matter for very delicate negotiation between the hotel and the con committee; one must not demand too much, for the hotel will turn very sticky if the registration turns out less than anticipated. (Ours was *more* than we'd guessed; the hotel treated the con committee accordingly.)

Make ye not the mistake of underestimating the hotel management. You can feel absolutely sure that deep within the recesses of the Convention Manager's desk he has a fat file folder marked "World Science Fiction." From this folder, if you are so lucky, he can furnish you with the most minute and detailed statistics: tips to the attendants in the Men's Room; number of martinis consumed Friday night in the Bellevue-Stratford bar; tips to the maids Saturday night in the Alexandria. He also has very precise charts and graphs about attendance, minimum and maximum expenditure per delegate, etc. He can, to the penny, tell you how much was spend last year at the Statler-Hilton in Washington, and how much will be spent next year in London. Every major metropolitan hotel has this file on hand, just waiting (and eagerly faunching) for your group to walk in and say, "Duh, we wanna put on a convention." This is particularly true of the hotel chains, but the grapevine between managements of the various hotels covers every possible facet of our conventions.

It is also necessary to make very careful and often-checked arrangements on just how the hotel is going to set up the ballroom for the costume ball. The safest thing is to, somehow, have somebody not only read the internal instructions the hotel will distribute to the room-arranging people, but also have somebody casually there when the various ramps and so on are being positioned and connected together in the ball room. For example: the platform on which the masqueraders at the Discon paraded was about four feet high. As originally planned by the hotel, the far end of the platform dropped off sheer, and their stairs down were off to one side. By just asking nicely, I got the hotel crew to put up a railing at the end of the platform so that the costume contestants, with vision limited by their costumes, didn't fall.

And then there is the matter of the banquet. We originally planned an evening banquet, but the expected price, about $7.50 to $7.90, was so high that we reconsidered and arranged for an afternoon luncheon banquet instead. The time was rather inconvenient, since it broke up the day's program, but the price was much cheaper — about $4.95 — and as a result, we got a very good turnout for the banquet (442). The food, and the menu, was very nearly as good as if we'd chosen an evening affair.

A word about the pricing of banquet tickets — which is simple, but not obvious unless you know it already. Take a moderately but not unduly pessimistic estimate of the banquet attendance, to begin with. (Include the free tickets, too. DC reckoned here just GoH, Toastmaster, and the wives of these two. Seattle figured *all* head-table banquet speakers except that the committee pays first and then takes a refund *if* finances warrant this.) Reckon the menu price, plus tax if any, plus a 13–15% tip (it varies from place to place) on the total. Divide by the estimated paid attendance, and round off to the best safe desirable figure. Even dollars is best, even halves next, quarters if you gotta, but it's silly to get into having to make nickles & dimes change on it. Any gain over your pessimistic guess increases your margin of safety, of course, and improves the Committee's chances to collect a well-deserved free meal.

Second of our Crafty Tricks: how to get the hotel to provide a choice of two entrees no matter how much they scream about this. The Discon had to give this up in trade for some other point, but it has — when you can get it — the advantage of catching the member's attention on the lower price even though he buys the higher one; further, it helps on the sales-cutoff problem. You merely pick one item that is also OK for general dining room sales, and then give them their early cutoff on the *other* item. At least, that's the way it worked in Seattle. it's a double-ended benefit, after all: you sell it to *them* as a way around the cutoff problem, and everybody is happy, except the Catering Director. [Catering Directors are never happy. It's an occupational requirement.]

About ticket sales: some hotels demand a guarantee of how many will attend the banquet, and they want the guarantee well in advance. This guarantee business has been the ruin of one convention (the Nycon II), and cost one of the Worldcons held in Philadelphia a good bit of money, too. Only advice we can give is to take the matter of whether the hotel demands an early guarantee into account when choosing the hotel. (And get that bit of information from the hotel manager himself. [Actually, the hotel manager's word is enough; the catering manager will kick and scream, but he is outranked by the hotel manager, and will have to fulfil the manager's promises. *Provided* they are on paper. And you keep your own copy . . . they tend to lose theirs. Honest-type loss.]) If need be, explain to the hotel management just what your situation is, and try to get the hotel to pick a number itself. It's a financial disaster to the con committee if you give a guarantee and can't meet it. On the other hand, if people just *won't* buy their banquet tickets early, then it'll have to be their hard luck if you're sold out.

Even if you do have to turn away late requests for tickets unsatisfied, console yourself with the thought that you've made things that much easier for the following con: people turned away will be damn sure to buy tickets in time at the next con. Traditionally, science fiction fans just won't send in banquet ticket money well in advance (we only had 73, a measly 17% of the final sales). Possibly it would help a bit if in your progress reports you announce that you will refund ticket money for all who get word to you before the hotel's cutoff time (which you'll have to announce then, of course) that they can't come.

There is some disagreement among con-chairmen and such knowledgeable folk about the whole idea of accommodating the hotel on guarantees — Devore recommends flat refusal to give *any* guarantee. Busby advises people to meet the guarantee question by saying you will guarantee, at any time, only the number of tickets sold, and emphasizing that all SFcons have a large share of last-minute buyers. If the hotel still insists on an early cutoff, go along with it and *publicize* it. You can't do much more. Somehow, the hotels always seem to relax and become more flexible at the last minute, but don't count on it.

And, the final matter to get set with the hotel: tell them exactly when and where you plan to start registration. That's usually been the afternoon of the day before the con properly starts.

The *scheduling* of the Banquet and the Costume Ball should also be mentioned specifically. In a hotel with more than one major hall available to you, this is no problem. But if Banquet, Ball, and the works have to go in the same hall, you must schedule so as to minimize the number of setups required of the hotel — and allow time for them, from "theatre type" seating to the separate arrangements required by the Ball and Banquet, and vice versa. Seacon did this by having the Ball Saturday night and the Banquet Sunday afternoon, making a total of four setups including the initial one. Almost any other arrangement would have required two additional setups. You have to try to make it as easy on the hotel as possible, after all; and setups cost them m*o*n*e*y.

Still remember one other thing: no matter how hard you go after free (or nominally-priced) Convention facilities, low flat Convention room-rates, low-priced banquet, and choice of entrees — not to mention fringe benefits such as see-no-evil houserichards and all-night coffee-shop/elevator service — you will never win *all* of those things. The committee's job is to get the best overall situation possible and to judge where to give and where to hold for the combined good of the Convention and the attending membership. The one Seattle lost, for instance, was the fight to get a $9 singles rate so as to have one 1-digit price on the hotel card. (For the same psychological reasons mentioned in the case of the two-entree banquet ticket.) The hotel *has* to make money; the Committee has to make this easy first on the Con's finances and next on the attendee's pocket. Of course, the attendee blows his savings in the bar, but that's *his* problem.

Up to this point, we've been talking about preparations, and in addition we've been talking in generalities. Now, we'll take up specifics as to what happened at Discon (will it be known some day as Discon I?), and how we think we *should* have handled our problems.

0.9 REGISTRATION

The last thing we mentioned under the general heading of preparations is to tell the hotel exactly when registration is to begin. You might as well expect that the hotel will post a beginning time for registration which indicates a few hours earlier than you expected. This happened to Chicon III; it happened, to a lesser degree, to the Discon. The only way to cope with the problem is to set up registration earlier than the time you told the hotel. This was only the first of many times when we set up things, hoping for the best, but prepared for the worst.

Registration itself is an affair where good layout of materials and lots of manpower are essential. Here, as in many other instances, lots of willing hose-carriers are very, very much needed. We got help, in the form of a billing typewriter [a typewriter with an extra-large type face, for typing the name badges] and an experienced typist to operate it, from the convention bureau of the local Chamber of Commerce. (The typist had been at the registration desks of hundreds of conventions; her help and advice were valuable.)

Your local convention bureau will furnish you with many valuable pieces of throw-away literature, advice, assistance, etc. However, the operation of convention bureaus fluctuates widely from city to city. Don't make the mistake of assuming that *all* their services are free to you. Some bureaus, for instance, will send a representative with you to the current year's convention to help you buy drinks and present your bid, free of charge to you. Some bureaus will even furnish all the registration clerks you need, for no charge; while others will expect $3.75 per hour, per clerk. Check first; it may save you embarrassment later. But do take advantage of all their free services.

A serious problem with registration is that it goes on throughout some of the more interesting parts of the convention program. After the initial flurry of activity on the evening preceding the first day of the con and the morning of the con itself had died down, registration could generally be handled by one or two people for the rest the first day, Saturday, and by about one person for the morning and early afternoon of the second day, Sunday.

Registration is something that is noticed mostly if it's bad; if we kept our waiting lines down to a reasonable point, we considered ourselves successful. Our preparations helped: we typed out name cards for everybody who had joined the convention in advance. As a result, we only had to prepare cards for the people who joined the con for the first time at the registration desk — about 225. Because of the $2/$3 membership fee system, there was some extra work; every pre-joiner's record card had to be checked to see if he owed another $1 or nay. Selling banquet tickets created some additional work, too, but not enough more to be a problem.

One matter that could have been a serious worry on our part proved to be none at all because of a bit of foresight on the part of our Treasurer. Bill Evans brought $460 in small bills and coin. About $100 was in $2 bills; these turned out to be especially useful in making change. It's amazing how much easier it is to count out two $2 bills than four $1 bills when breaking a $5, or making change in dozens of other ways. Bill now feels he should have had a larger part of his change money in

$2s. [Aside from the convenience, don't forget the propaganda element. If you're distributing infrequently-used money like $2 bills or silver cartwheels, you are reminding every hotel worker who gets one that you are a Welcome Guest.] Another point of importance: if the banquet tickets are $something.75, have about as many quarters available as you expect to sell banquet tickets, since a large portion of the registrants will buy odd-price items like this with an even handful of bills.

(At night, of course, the accumulated cash and checks — which amounted at the end of the con to about $4,000 — was a*l*w*a*y*s stored in the hotel safe. When the accumulation was finally deposited, the Tuesday after the con, a group of six of us went to the bank to guard the green stuff on its way.)

While your space problems will probably be different from ours, we found the most efficient system was to establish two lines — one for new registrants, one for the pre-registered — with *one* person in the center, handling the tickets and the cashbox.

In addition to the membership badge, the program book, and the banquet tickets, we also had a goodly handful of other stuff to give out at registration; copies of *The Castle of Iron,* donated by Pyramid Books; various pocketbooks from Regency Books; and a fair-sized bundle of monster magazines. Chicon III solved this problem by stuffing a big bag full of the various hand-out items. This would have been a good idea for us, too; we considered it, but just never got around to doing it beforehand. Instead, we simply spread out the gift items on the registration tables, and told the delegates to take one of each.

0.10 THE AUCTION

In past cons, the auction was all that stood between the financial success of the con and bankruptcy. Thanks to the $3 membership fee, this is no longer the case. For our con, the Discon, the auction served to finance the *Proceedings*; it was extra income, not essential income.

The Discon had made a limited request for auction

material; we only had about 150 items for the auction-eers. These, however, included some very high-value items: two Emsh color paintings, a Rogers painting in frame, several Rogers black&white illos, an electric Gestetner duplicator, and a Roy Krenkel painting.

Unfortunately, I had miscalculated the time needed for the auction. The auctioneers, Ed Wood and Steve Tolliver, had only about 90 minutes, scattered throughout the con, to dispose of our items. We set up a display of auction material in a side room, the first day of the con, with many of the items available for over-the-table sale at fixed prices — small b&w's and suchlike. The basic idea of disposing of items of low value in this was is a good one; pieces of only moderate distinction can be moved this way with minimum delay to the con as a whole.

But this was one of the things we didn't have time to carry through adequately.

We *did* find time to make out a list of all auction items which were available to us before the con; each item was numbered, tagged, and identified on the list. (And we had a couple of footlockers — with ~~foot~~locks — for storing the material between whiles; these took a good bit of worry off the committee.)

To the auctioneers we gave the instructions: sell the color paintings, the Freas and Lawrence material, the Gestetner, the Rogers material, Tolkein books, and certain manuscripts at the highest prices you can get; sell the rest at whatever price will enable you to distribute as much of it as possible to whoever wants to buy. Thus, money was an object only with a limited number of items; availability to members of the con was an object with the rest.

The auctioneers came through magnificently. We netted about $500 on the auction, almost entirely from the major items; we managed to sell virtually every item we had available for auction, with the exception of a few Rogers and Lawrence illos which were not bringing high enough bids.

To dispose of 150 items in three or four sessions totalling about 90 minutes is quite a feat; our greatest appreciation to Ed Wood and Steve Tolliver for managing this.

Their usual procedure was to alternate. Ed is a boisterous, stout, energetic chap with a — err — carrying voice. Steve is long, lanky, easy-going, and soft-spoken. While the audience was recovering from Ed's impact, Steve would bounce up to the microphone and start to auction off an item. As soon as it was sold, Ed would bounce back with a yell. This sort of two-man system worked well at Chicago, too, with Al (West Coast) Lewis and Marty Moore. We recommend it highly. [Fortunately, with this pair, we could handle things by giving basic instructions to the auctioneers and, from then on, letting them decide what went. Many of their questions the committee answered with a "do it the way you think best."]

Note that this was not strictly a two-man show. There were also two to four of the Committee and the assistant hose-carriers working on the auction most of the time. The Treasurer or Secretary — sometimes both — were always there to help collect and record the money (the auction list, again, was helpful here) and to make the necessary change. (and have *plenty* of small change!!) These others helped by answering questions, pushing the crowd back when things got too crowded, picking out the next items to be auctioned, and so on. The setup and takedown time for an auction is not inconsiderable; we erred in not realizing and allowing for this; the number of volunteer assistants saved us from more trouble than we had.

Incidentally, the District of Columbia has a sales tax. Auction material, like everything else sold through the con committee, was subject to this tax. Therefore, we had to compute the tax on every sale (3%), make change in odd pennies, and prepare a final report to the District of Columbia government.

All in all, we feel that the auction was a success, largely because the auctioneers carried out their instructions so well. It would have been a better auction if we'd allowed more time; had made and publicized a pre-auction display of material; and carried through the arrangements for greater across-the-table sale of the less valuable of the illos and manuscripts.

And a final note: while prices and demand for black & white illos have been declining for some time now, the interest in story manuscripts is remarkably high. Future con committees will do well to seek manuscripts out — always being careful, of course, not to flood the market and saturate demand. More generally, it is well to avoid saturating the market on any item. If you have material that's not worth the trouble of auctioning off, store it away, pass it along, store it, or junk it — but, for goodness' sake, don't clutter up your precious convention time trying to auction material off for a nickel or a dime.

I. THE PROGRAM: THE FIRST DAY

In retrospect, we know we overprogrammed. Chicon III scheduled about 17+ hours of program and auction (exclusive of banquet and ball). We originally aimed at 10 hours, but Fascinating Things kept turning up, and we wound up with a trifle over 13 hours (again, exclusive of banquet and ball). 13+ hours would fit nicely into a four-day convention (it might fit into a three-day con with an evening banquet) but, as it was, things were pretty tight. That we were on time so much was because of the outstanding co-operation on the part of the speakers, a grim determination on the part of the chairman to stay on schedule, and the fact that his watch was running three minutes fast. (Why stay on time? For the simple reason that people who don't want to watch *all* of the program would like to know when to be back to see the bits they are interested in.)

The program started on time, but not before I nearly had kittens. The start was scheduled at 12:30, and at 12:00 another group started filing into the Congressional Room; the 315th Infantry, or some such. Luckily, the hotel functionary who was in charge of conventions was on hand, and was able to assure us that the strangers would be out on time. They were, though just barely.

I spent the intervening half-hour making arrangements for the opening item. I had brought two swords, Joe Mayhew had brought another, John Boardman had his magician's costume handy, and Fritz Leiber and L. Sprague de Camp were willing, so all was set.

At exactly 12:30, Saturday, the 31st of August 1963, I tapped the gavel to open the 21st World Science Fiction Convention. Hardly anyone paid attention; you know how slow the initial chatter is to quiet down. I hammered with the gavel, then pounded. No one particularly noticed. So — the pre-arranged signal — I pointed the gavel to my right.

Instantly, Sprague and Fritz started yelling at each other in Persian and Old English. They jumped to their feet, still spouting abuse and archaic curses, grabbed a sword apiece, and started fencing. That *did* get the crowd's attention. After a few moments of sword-clashing, I pointed my gavel to my left, in another pre-arranged signal. John Boardman, attired in black robe, tall conical wizard's cap, and a long black beard, stepped out from behind a pillar of the room, pointed a sword, and began to read an authentic incantation from a Grimoire. The swordsmen stopped to watch, and then — as soon as the crowd's attention shifted to the magician — sat down. Finally, the incantation ended, Boardman stepped behind the pillar again, I tapped the gavel, and *this* time I had complete silence. I announced that the convention was in session, reminded people that they'd need their Owl-and-Saturn name badges to get into the costume ball that evening, and introduced Jim Blish.

The spectacular beginning was very worth while. It got the crowd's attention, so that the first speaker could speak without interference; and, more than that, it sort of gave notice that things had started off with a ~~ba~~ clang — and with the chairman definitely in control. This, I suspect, helped as things went on.

We tried another bit but didn't carry through on it: at the Detention, the con committee wore striped blazers, giving the con members an easy means of identifying the officials. We tried a similar stunt: white lab coats. Most of us abandoned them after half an hour. It is well for the con committee to be readily identifiable — not only so that you can readily be found by con members in need, but also so you can find *each other* quickly in a crowd. Then, too, it makes it plainer, when one of the committee makes an announcement, that it *is* one of the committee speaking.

Anyway, Jim Blish began to speak, right on schedule. Unfortunately he wasn't feeling well and had to take a break before he'd finished. Luckily, Dick Eney was on the speaker's platform at that moment, too, so one member of the committee could tend to this problem while the other — me — dashed off to set up the next program item.

This was one that had been invented by Bob Silverberg, although he hadn't realized it at the time. He had remarked (I think at one of the Disclaves) that he'd long wanted to do an article about the hazards of doing stories to fit illustrations instead of the other way around. Several letters and a couple of phone calls had finally persuaded him to be on a two-man panel on the subject, provided that Ed Emsh was on it too. Ed was willing, so "Ring Around an Illustration" was on the program, scheduled for 1:30. Unfortunately, here it was 1:00 — and, though Silverberg was available, Emsh wasn't in sight. Luckily for me, Fritz Leiber was sitting in the front row — had, indeed, planned to add a few remarks from the floor about his own experience. I asked him to substitute for Emsh, he said OK, and the panel was on.

Bob spoke first about his experiences in writing stories to fit illustrations — usually cover paintings — which had been done before the story had been thought up. By the time he was ready to turn and ask for Fritz' comments, I had located Emsh and had gotten him up on the platform, ready to speak. Bob was not a little surprised at this.

The talk turned out to be a very successful one; it was largely extemporaneous, and all three participants visibly had fun with it. Let me say something about the panel idea at this point, and something else about the situation we had at the time.

First, the two-man panel (or three-man panel, as this one turned out to be) is a highly effective method of presenting a subject. It avoids both the dullness of listening to but one speaker and also the somewhat disjointed effect of a very large panel. A two man panel often breaks out into more spontaneous conversation than any of the other type of program items. I recommend it highly to future cons.

Second, it is very important that the con committee be so organized that the principal programmer (who is not necessarily the chairman, though in our case he was) is virtually always in the main program hall, free of other duties, so that he can cope with whatever comes up. In our case, the presence of two committee members in the

The PROGRAM

Congressional Room, unless otherwise indicated.

<u>Time</u>   <u>Place</u>

Saturday

9:00am Registration   <u>Upper Lobby</u>

12:30pm Opening of the DisCon

12:45   Jim Blish:
        AN ANSWER OF SORTS

1:30   Bob Silverberg & Ed Emsh:
        RING AROUND AN ILLUSTRATION
        Problems in writing a story around an illo;
        or, pleasing editor's whimsy for fun and profit.

2:00   Ted Cogswell & Cohorts:
        HIPPOCRENE AND HYPERSPACE
        Cogswell struggles with the Muses, best two
        falls out of three.

2:30   Introduction of notables, auction, and break.

3:15   Larry Ivie & Dick Lupoff:
        SF ILLUSTRATION & ART IN THE COMIC BOOKS
        (Me to Your Leader Take)
        All in color for a dime: the rise and fall of
        the comic book.

4:30   Willy Ley:
        MYSTERIES OF ASTRONOMY
        A spring day on Pluto, and such.

7:30   The Convention Members: <u>Presidential</u>
        THE COSTUME BALL [<u>Admission</u> <u>by</u> <u>badge</u>]
        Scenes to numb the senses and appall the mind,
        with music by Ira Sabin and his Orch.
        - - - - - - - - - - - - - - - -

Sunday

11:00am Burroughs Bibliophiles:
        DUM-DUM
        Tarzan Rides Again.

11:00   Fantasy Amateur Press Association: <u>California</u>
        Annual THROW THE RASCALS OUT meeting.

12:30pm Fumio Suzuki via Dick Lupoff:
        ASTRO BOY
        A Japanese s-f cartoon film in English.

1:00   Hyborian Legion:
        MUSTER
        de Camp and his cohorts on Conan.

2:00   The Convention Members: <u>Presidential</u>
        BANQUET LUNCHEON
        Guest of Honor: Will F. Jenkins [Murray Leinster]
        Toastmaster: Isaac Asimov. Hugos.

5:30pm   L. Sprague de Camp, Isaac Asimov, Willy Ley,
         Ed Emsh, and Fritz Leiber
            WHAT SHOULD A BEM LOOK LIKE?
6:30   Seabury Quinn:
            SCIENCE FICTION VERSUS FANTASY
            The difference in treatment of a theme.
7:00   Auction and intermission.
7:30   The Convention Members:
            THE ANNUAL BUSINESS MEETING
            Presentation of special awards. Reports of
            Committees. Choice of site for the 1964
            Convention.
8:00   Don Wollheim, Dick Lupoff, Sam Moskowitz:
            SWORDS AGAINST EDGAR RICE BURROUGHS
            Alan Howard will moderate this affair.
9:00   Juanita Coulson, Ted White, D&M Thompson:
            DE STIJL MIT DE STYLUS
            The art of putting art on stencil and
            other aspects of good mimeography.
            - - - - - - - - - - - - - -

         Monday

11:30am Auction
12:00n   John Campbell, Don Wollheim, A.J. Budrys,
         Cele Goldsmith:
            THE EDITORS SPEAK
            Fred Pohl moderates this discussion of
            the problems of the editor.
1:00pm   Barbara Silverberg, Elsie Wollheim, Carol
         Pohl, and others:
            LIFE WITH A STF WRITER
            Ted Cogswell has induced the wives to tell
            their side of the story.
1:30   Intermission
1:45   Hal Clement & P. Schuyler Miller:
            IS THE SF STORY A MENTAL EXERCISE?
            Hal says it is, like a detective story.
2:15   Judy Merril and Fritz Leiber, with aid:
            SKIT
            They've whipped up something, but won't
            tell us.
2:45   George Scithers, Ben Stark, Earl Kemp:
            THE FOURTH CONVENTION
            [You thought there were only three, didn't you?]

And for last minute changes and additions . . .
         Bulletin Board
            In the Upper Lobby, just outside Foyer Number 2.

I. THE PROGRAM: THE FIRST DAY   45 hall when an emergency came up was what enabled us to keep the program going without any real lapse. The presence of willing assistants, who eventually found Emsh and shooed him on-stage, was also very important. But the reason we had people available mustn't be overlooked: we had other committee members available to take care of registration, of questions, of continued arrangements with the hotel management, and of all the other things which have to be taken care of while the program is going on.

The Silverberg/Emsh/Leiber panel finished at about 1:40, leaving us (as Wally Weber has put it) ahead of schedule for the first time in convention history. Luckily, I had arranged with Katherine MacLean beforehand for such an eventuality; she had volunteered to speak as a fill-in for any desired length of time. While the S/E/L panel was winding up, I asked Katherine if she'd get us back on schedule, she asked Lester del Rey if he'd help too, and then both accepted. Katherine spoke on the High Art & Mysterie of people-guiding, Lester agreed with her on some points and disagreed on others, and then, thanks to the pair's willingness to take the platform and speak entertainingly on practically no notice at all, we were back on schedule again.

The next item on the program was Cogswell's "Hippocrene and Hyperspace" — an idea of Ted's, from one of the parties at Chicon III. (Ted professes not to remember thinking of it, suggesting he might have been drunk at the time. *In vino . . .*) Anyway, I'd checked the idea out with a few pros, and they said, yes, they *did* have some bits of poetry they'd composed and put in the back of their file cabinets for lack of an audience or a market. And some said, yes, they'd be glad to read them at the Discon. I remembered the idea rather late in the summer and phoned Ted; he immediately contacted a number of the pros, and Gordon R Dickson, L Sprague de Camp, Jim Blish, and Fritz Leiber accepted. In making up the program book, the committee deliberately hid the nature of the program item under a confusing title; the subtitle was "Cogswell struggles with the Muse, best two falls out of three." Reason? We were afraid that a bald announcement that we were going to have a poetry-reading session would scare off the audience. As it was, the poems were enjoyed, and everyone, I think, got a little extra pleasure from the sheer uncommonness of the feature.

Following the poetry session, Jim Blish came back in fine style. His basic thesis — with barbed instances — was that literary criticism on this side of the Atlantic is simply awful, while the British reviewers are still highly skilled craftsmen.

Next came one of the shortest introductions of noteables on record. I stood at the podium and introduced the handful of pros and fans whom I could recognize from where I stood. Then a short, short auction period, a few more minutes to introduce the Guest of Honor, Will F Jenkins, and some of his family — and the program was back on schedule again.

There was a special reason for preoccupation with the schedule this afternoon: Larry Ivie and Dick Lupoff had had their time trimmed from the 90 minutes they had material for, to 75 minutes; Willy Ley had 60 minutes of material to cover in 60 minutes; and at the scheduled end of *his* talk, we had to clear the hall for another group.

The first of these talks, "SF Illustration and Art in the Comic Books," was actually two talks: one by Larry Ivie, stressing artistic styles in the illustrative fields, and one by Dick Lupoff, covering the plots and characters of the comic books of a few decades ago. Both talks were illustrated by slides which had been prepared by Phil Harrell. (An extra blessing for the con committee: the two speakers took turns running the slide projector, so we didn't have to worry about *that* bit.)

The projector used was rented from a reliable local firm. For about $70 we got a movie projector, a 35mm slide projector, a screen, and a helpful chap who showed us how to use the stuff. (There were also extra projector bulbs provided; though we didn't need them, we were glad to have them handy.) Though 75 minutes is a bit long for a slide lecture, even with two lecturers, the content of the program and the interest of the audience kept things going. At the end of the talk Dick Lupoff, who spoke second, got a very sticky question from the audience: Will Sykora asked Dick if Dr. Wertham wasn't right in denouncing comic books as the source of all evil. Dick neatly fielded this by explaining that the chairman of the con (loveable me) had threatened dire disaster if he spoke overtime, so . . .

The comics lecture was one of the best ideas I had in setting up the program. It was invented for two reasons. First, interest in old comic book heroes had reached sort of a peak in the year or so previous to the con, and thus the time was appropriate for a con program item on the subject; second, the costume ball very likely would have comic book heroes among the costumes, and the lecture would serve as sort of an introduction. Dick Lupoff pointed out that something over 400 comic book heroes of some importance had been invented and illustrated, so the chance of his showing a hero who would also appear at the ball was low. No matter; the talk was fun.

Willy Ley is one of those people who is interesting, no matter how many times one hears him. We gave him a free hand to pick his subject, and then tried to title his talk with something that would fit whatever he said. Willy is truly a professional lecturer; he is interesting, informative, versatile, and can fit his talk exactly into an allotted time. No convention should be without him.

II. THE COSTUME BALL

The costume ball has become, over twenty-five years, an almost indispensable part of the World Science Fiction Convention. It is also one of the most expensive items on the con committee's budget, if they choose live music, which is horribly expensive. Unfortunately, the judging has at times in the past generated some very nasty feuds afterwards.

In view of some of the sillier charges made about the judging at Seacon, the Discon committee made choice of judges and determination of categories one of the earliest items of business. Choice of categories was checked out with members of previous con committees and with the general readership of *Shangri L'Affaires,* the LASFS fanzine. [Any regular large-circulation fanzine would have done; picking the LASFS organ was a ploy. Elements of the LASFS had been the noisiest objectors to SeaCon's arrangements, though this partly traced to a personal feud.] Based on the remarks we got in reply, particularly the suggestions made by Robert Bloch, the Discon chose a mixture of specified and open categories: Most Beautiful Costume, Most Authentic Fantasy Costume, Most Authentic Science Fiction Costume, Most BEMish Costume, and three Judges' Choice categories — *a, alpha,* and *aleph.* The Most Beautiful Costume was intended for actual costuming, of course, not (as sometimes before) for Best Undressed. The Most Authentic categories were for portrayal of specific characters from The Literature, and the Most BEMish was intended for — well, you know what I mean by BEMish, I hope. The open categories were for whatever three costumes the judges chose, and for whatever reasons they specified.

The reason for complexity and vagueness was this: the four specified categories gave potential contestants something to plan for ahead of time; the open categories allowed the judges to award for excellence and originality in whatever way they wanted, and avoided the dilemma of having *two* superlative costumes which might both be described as "Best Fantasy" or whatever. Finally, we tried to avoid the bitterness over the eligibility of groups (the basis of the nastiness after Seacon) by announcing, in advance, that (1) groups, as groups, were eligible for any of the awards given, and (2) the *individuals* in each group were also eligible for individual awards if they wished to be.

As for the judges: we thought that a very good candidate for such a position would be someone who had worn a particularly spectacular costume the previous year, giving him the chance to relax for *this* year. Unfortunately, some of our first choices on this basis turned out not to be available; Bjo Trimble, Al Lewis, and the Shaws. Of the people we had carefully asked in advance, only the

Lupoffs (who were pretty spectacular in some of their previous appearances) managed to get to the con. During the first day, therefore, I asked Jim Warren, Fritz Leiber, 4e Ackerman, J. Ben Stark, and Ed Emsh to be judges. All accepted; the Lupoffs, though, were to act as a single judge.

By the way, in picking judges, try for diversity. Properly, a set of judges should represent whatever interests are current in fandom, as well as the general stream of fantasy and science fiction. For the Discon, we had a comics fan, a publisher of a monster magazine, a writer of fantasy *and* science fiction, and two other fans who, I hoped, would have the sort of practicality that would get the overall group into a reasonably quick decision. Certainly, any ideal panel should have a woman on it, as well as an artist. But just *who*? . . . well, picking a panel is one of the things that make running a convention fun.

The next big problem was arranging the ball room. We were lucky to have an entirely cooperative hotel management to deal with. We asked for, and got, a runway about eight feet wide, running almost the length of the big Presidential ballroom (itself 110 by 94 feet), with a ramp leading up to the runway at one end, and a sort of extension sticking out of the middle of the ramp toward the center of the room. The runway and its extension (looking from above like a very wide letter T) were about four feet off the ballroom floor. The only thing we didn't get was a down ramp off the far end of the platform; we had to use a short stair instead. For announcements we obtained a hand-held microphone plus one floor microphone. The room itself had about twenty or so tables scattered about the floor for those who wanted to sit.

We had originally planned to have a couple of bars dispensing hard liquors as well as beer and wine; in fact, we'd scheduled the ball for Saturday to allow this — the drinking laws in D.C. were barbarically rigid, allowing practically nothing on Sunday. However, the hotel management panicked at the last minute, when it finally sank in how many under-eighteen-year-olds would be at the ball, and limited the bars to soft drinks. Oddly enough, the lack of lubrication didn't seem to hurt the ball any, as far as we could see.

Since we had a runway for displaying the costumes, and since we had microphone facilities, we arranged a procedure for announcing the costumes. This procedure we announced early and often. For the contestants, it consisted of taking a printed slip of paper (available from registration and at the ball); printing on the slip the name of the costume, the source (story, book, series, or whatever) of the character depicted, and the name of the costume wearer; and wearing the slips on or near the left shoulder when they entered the ballroom. (Individuals had white paper slips; groups had additional red slips for the leader to carry.) In addition to announcing this beforehand, we had a number of assistants on the ballroom floor with extra slips and straight pins for fastening them on. 'Tis a good thing we did, too; we recommend you do likewise if you adopt a similar system.

Then there was the question: shall we have live music? Like many big cities, Washington is solidly tied up by the musicians' union, which not only dictates what rates you will pay each musician, but also how many musicians you must hire. This depends on volume; for the big Presidential room, this came to nine musicians, which meant something over $350. This led to what I think was our biggest error in putting on the costume ball: we got the band at the last minute. Here is how it happened:

Until about two months before the convention itself, we weren't sure that we could afford to spend the $300 and something for music. Wen we finally did decide, there wasn't enough time for lengthy searching. None of the committee had enough spare time during those last two months to really deal with the musicians the way we should have. What we *did* do was to engage a regular (though versatile) dance band, Ira Sabin and His Orchestra, and tell the band leader to try and think up appropriate snatches of music for the usual costume types: futuristic, gruesome, sexy, heroic, and so on. The difficulty was that popular and show music has a certain sameness to it: a group of musicians familiar with the classical repertoire would have been better able to match a bit of music to each costume as it went by.

You see, the principal object in *having* a band for our costume ball was to provide fanfares and, most important, to provide snatches of appropriate music for each contestant as he/she/whatever paraded by on the elevated runway. Providing music for dancing was strictly secondary. In retrospect, the best possible group of musicians for such a purpose would be a string quartet plus a few wind instruments (say, a flute, oboe, and trumpet) and a good percussion man. The reason for such an odd selection is that for backgrounding a costume without drowning out the announcer, a variety of single instruments is better than an orchestra playing all together. Further (and this is more important than you might think) it's considerably quicker for (say) a violinist to be told, "you play something for this next costume" and to begin than for the orchestra leader to be told, to decide what to play, and to go, no matter how quickly, through the "a-one, a-two, a-three . . ." routine. We used single instruments as background and fanfare for a couple of the costumes at the Discon; this worked well, and I wish we'd done more of it.

As for the matter of controlling entry to the ball, the hotel management strongly advised us to get a detective agency to send us a uniformed guard. Reason? To keep non-SF-convention folk from crashing the affair. We found the local agency charged only $2 per hour (minimum: five hours). We planned to get two guards, but due to a mixup only got one. Believe us, it was worth it. There were three doors to the ballroom; we closed one, put the guard at the door closest to the incoming crowds, and manned the remaining door with some of our people, Chick Derry and Phil Bridges. Dick Eney lurked nearby with a handful of membership cards, name badges, and banquet tickets. We had announced several times that only people with either name badges (which were given out at registration, one per registered member) or costumes too elaborate to carry a badge with convenience would be allowed in.

Even on a purely financial basis, the guard was very worth while. He cost us $10, while Dick took in a bit over $40 in memberships and tickets which he sold at the door. Also, while the Chicon III committee estimates that about 100 more folk attended the ball than paid for membership, we estimate that not more than a dozen did at the Discon. The problem of outsiders crowding into the ball to the exclusion of the convention members simply didn't happen. With the exception of a press photographer, the band, and hotel employees, nobody got in (and stayed in) except members of the con, and two ingenious porch-climbers.

We scheduled the ball for 7:30 P.M. At 8:00 P.M., I was still trying to round up the judges. Ackerman had disappeared completely, so I grabbed Bob Leman, the heralds managed to get the rest together in one spot, and we were ready to begin.

A word of explanation here. The band was sitting on the runway — about in the middle, against the wall. We had chairs on the runway extension, which stuck out into the audience area, for the judges. The announcer's mike was at the foot of the ramp that led up to the runway proper. At the far end of the runway was a set of stairs leading down to floor level. Beyond that, the end of the room was screened with a curtain. Now, by a prearrangement known only to me, Bill Evans, and Larry Breed, we had hired a bagpiper (complete with kilts and other accessories) who was at that moment waiting behind the curtain. I told the judges what was about to happen, and signaled to Larry.

In a few seconds, the bagpiper came from behind the curtain and ascended the stairs. Hardly anyone noticed he was there — until he began to play. After that, hardy anyone noticed anything else. The piper, still marching, marched the length of the runway to the judges, who were waiting in a little group. Turning, he piped the judges to their seats on the runway extension, faced them and piped a final tune ("Garry Owen"), and then left amid applause.

Then the costume parade began. This was the procedure. A herald would bring an individual or a group to the announcer. The announcer would take the contestant's identity slip, signal to the band leader to play. The band leader would decide on a theme and begin, while the announcer started the contestant up the ramp and announced the name of the costume and the source of the character, when there was one. The contestant walked (or slithered, or whatever) on past the judges. Once past, the announcer read the contestant's name, which was the prearranged signal for the contestant to skedaddle, and reached for the next contestant's identity slip.

Since groups paraded both as groups and then as individuals, the heralds got all the groups through the parade early. And, to provide a good balance, the heralds and the announcer worked together to pick contrasting costumes for successive entries. A BEM followed by a beauty, a group followed by an individual. As for the slips, as the announcer finished with each, he handed it to little Betty Berg, who scurried over to the judges. They used the slips to mark their comments on as an aid to the judging.

There were a few folk, including members of the committee, who didn't want to be judged, but who did want to show off costumes. These were announced in the usual way, but the slips were simply not forwarded to the judges.

As far as the announcing system went, there could have been improvements. In particular, the announcer would have been better placed in the center of the runway, among the orchestra, so that the contestants passed between him and the judges. The advantage would have been that he could have worked more closely with the orchestra and the judges. With this change in position, the slips would have been delivered to the announcer, one by one, and he would have delivered them to the judges simply by taking a step forward and handing each slip across. The important value of the arrangement we had, I think, is that the judges and the audience were on the *same* side of the contestants, so the contestants turned their back to neither. Further, the slips did help the judging considerably, as well as making things a lot better for the announcer as well. And having heralds get contestants avoided the costume waiting line, always an awkward thing to manage. It also made it possible to put a final end to the bickering about groups by allowing people to compete both in groups *and* as individuals.

It took just short of an hour for our contestants to be shooed past the judges. Afterward, the judges retired behind the curtain, and the band played odds and ends. Then the judges reappeared with a handful of identity slips: the semi-finals. The announcer read off the names, to get them in a group at the beginning of the ramp, and then announced them one by one, letting them walk past the judges again, while the orchestra played appropriate bits of music. Again the judges retired, returning at last with just seven slips. The announcer called up the winners, and the judges presented the awards: 8x10 framed transparencies of drawings by Bjo Trimble.

One final thing which we overlooked: when the winners have been finally picked, and have gotten their prizes, it's very important that the winners be asked to pose for several minutes on the runway, for the benefit of the photographers.

And then the most extraordinary thing happened: when the band started to play dance music, s' help me, the audience began to dance. There was a fair crowd on the dance floor from the end of the judging until the band folded up at 11:00 P.M. In fact, there were probably more fans dancing than have seen since . . . well, for as long as I've been going to cons. The reason? Whatever the shortcomings of pop music as far as fanfares go, Ira Sabin is an expert when it comes to picking the music that his audience will dance to. We hadn't expected any real interest in dancing, extrapolating from the lack of dancing at previous cons; the band was primarily to provide background and continuity for the parade, plus fanfares for the judges when they came out to announce the winners. Instead . . .

There was only one almost-incident to mar things.

Gary Deindorfer brought two friends — not members of the con — into the ballroom by simply shoving past Derry and Bridges, with the explanation that they "were just going to see someone and would be right back out." When they didn't come out, Bridges went in to tell them to go. Deindorfer and Calvin Demmon told him to Go Away and Quit Bothering Them. Bridges asked Eney what to do; Eney matter-of-factly said, "get the guard to eject them." [Old proverb: "The OE is evil and his heart is Black."] Bridges got the guard, who quickly and quietly went to the group and murmured "you'll have to leave." They went, right then, without Word One of argument. The point has since been advanced by some Focal Points of Fandom that this ejection was wicked and sinful or something. Our opinion is that neither Deindorfer nor Demmon (nor, for that matter, anybody else) is Big Named enough, or Big Mouthed enough, to bull hiser way into the costume ball free.

We briefly considered having a uniformed guard at more sessions of the convention than just the costume ball, but abandoned the idea because it would be too much trouble. (Of course, the case of the Pacificon II, where a clique had given advance notice that it meant to try scuttling things, is a special one.) We advise strongly that future cons cover at least one important session (probably the costume ball) with a guard system, to allow in only those who have paid. Judging from our experience, the expense of a private detective agency's uniformed guard is very, very worthwhile. If the entrances to the room cannot be covered easily by one man, two are even better.

III. REST BREAK

Sunday morning was a time that pretty well ran itself: the Burroughs Bibliophiles and the Fantasy Amateur Press Association (two groups whose memberships have very little overlap — a factor to consider in scheduling simultaneous meetings) ran their own meetings, needing only meeting room space. The only problems with the meetings of various groups and societies are, to get them to tell you (in advance of the cutoff date for your scheduling) that they *do* want to meet, and to persuade them that their meetings will have to be scheduled in the morning, because all the prime evening program time is being scheduled for the general program items.

A cartoon film was provided by a friend of Dick Lupoff's. Dave van Arnam, another friend of Dick's, ran the projector. A typical last minute incident illustrates the need for buffer items throughout the program: Bhob Stewart called up a few days before the con to offer some extra film bits. We squeezed in an excellent experimental film by Bhob, and a sequence from an old movie which showed scenes straight out of Dante's Hell, marvellously effective. We didn't have time for a third film, because we had already scheduled another meeting (a Muster of the Hyborian Legion) in that room at 1:00 P.M. As it was, the Muster ran from 1:30 till 2:00 and had a second session the following morning.

And suddenly it was time for the Banquet and the Hugos.

VI. THE BANQUET

Without a doubt, the banquet represents more work, on the part of the con committee, than any other part of the convention.

The really big items are the preparations long beforehand. First, the whole of the Hugos; voting, preparation of the awards, trying to get the winners to the con without letting them know they've won . . . Another big item is the hotel arrangements for this; fixing a price and a menu, preparing Banquet tickets.

And then there's picking a Guest of Honor and a Toastmaster, getting them to come (of course, you tell *them* that they're supposed to be Guest of Honor and Toastmaster), and, if you're as cautious as we were, you'll pick out an alternate for each. (Our first choice on Guest of Honor, Will F. Jenkins, made it, but personal affairs called Ted Sturgeon away and Isaac Asimov did the toasts instead — and very well too — but more of that later.)

But that isn't all. During all the rush and confusion of registering people for the con, it's a good idea to keep tabs on the hotel room assignments too; it's customary for the con committee to provide a free room for the Guest of Honor at the con hotel. (If you're lucky, the room will be one provided free by the hotel to the committee.) However, *you've* got to get the Guest of Honor *into* that free room. Out problem was complicated: (1) none of the committee had ever met Will F. Jenkins, and (2) there is also a Philadelphia fan named Will *J.* Jenkins. The hotel almost put the wrong Jenkins in the complimentary room; only a visit by one of the committee and a casual question prevented a Ghastly Mistake.

And there's the sale of the banquet tickets. On this, were we lucky! Instead of asking a guarantee, the hotel — in the person of Mr. Tristano, the banquet manager — asked for our estimate of eventual ticket sales, and asked to be kept informed of how sales were going. Our estimates weren't very accurate; we guessed variously between 250 and 400.

However, through registration Saturday morning, Saturday afternoon, and Sunday morning, just about every two hours, we told Mr. Tristano what the total sales were at that point and asked "Shall we keep selling?" And he'd always smile and say yes. Eventually sales reached 442 — at least 50 sold in the last couple of hours — and Bill Evans even sold a few tickets at the door of the banquet itself.

Now, this isn't as simple as it sounds, really. Since the banquet is on a weekend, the hotel has to buy the food a few days in advance. And since a banquet is a large affair, a lot of waiters have to be notified a day or so in advance that they must show up. A lot of hotels will demand a guarantee; you guarantee that X tickets will be sold, and they'll (usually) agree to have X + 10% places set, in case you have a few more than the guarantee show up. In our case, the hotel made a guess of its own, and when our sales seemed to be heading for this figure, they let us keep selling. If sales had outrun the hotel's estimate (they had figured 447) we *would* have had to shut ticket sales off early.

Unfortunately for future cons, this sets a Bad Example to the con members. Fans have always expected to be able to get tickets at the last minute; this experience could reinforce the expectation — and for most cons and hotels, this simply won't be the case. I remind you again: the NYCon II went broke largely from guaranteeing to the hotel more tickets than were actually sold.

The Guest of Honor and his wife, and the Toastmaster, got free banquet tickets. Everyone else paid, including the committee. As for who sat at the head table? That we decided late Saturday night, as I remember. It was simply the basic, four man con committee, plus the hardest-working of our assistants. And, I might add, it is only during the con that you find out who, of the group that are supposed to be helping, actually are.

Let me stress that it is the assistants, the hose- and spear-carriers, that make it possible for a con to run *smoothly.* Certainly a con needs new and original ideas, but the people who think up the ideas must be the ones, by and large, who will carry them out. If the Discon had any success, it is in surprisingly large part due to people like Joe Sarno, Larry Breed, Steve Russell, George Mac-Mullin, Tom Rutherford, and Tom Haughey.

Anyway. We got all the head-tablers positioned. Larry Breed and Steve Russell (two folk from Stanford, California, who spent a week before the con Helping Out [and who were largely responsible for completing the Hugos] brought in a trunk containing the seven Hugos and the two plaques. They spread the Hugos out on a piano behind the head table (carefully covered) and we began to eat.

[About this time, things began to run themselves, and the release of pressure threw George into a brief tailspin. The rest of the committee, or at least Bill Evans and Dick Eney, who were close enough to notice what was happening, sprang to the rescue (nerved to't by the thought of having to tackle George's job, otherwise) and plied him with fortifying drinks until he perked up again. About three large glasses of milk, it took to do the fortifying. I'm afraid George doesn't read these conreports that explain what formidable guzzlers fans are . . .]

A word on scheduling: the banquet started at 2 P.M.; we had to clear the hall at 5 P.M. (It turned out our successors in the room were a pack of high school fraternity kids, who screamed their goddam little heads off for the rest of the evening.) We expected that there'd be just time for the banquet, the Guest of Honor speech, and the Hugos. Therefore, we had firmly removed all other award presentations to the Business Meeting.

Anyway, the food was brought on, people began to eat, and in due time they finished. That is: when the last waiter has delivered the last dessert, and the last table has had time to eat the dessert, and the general noise has gradually changed from dishes-and-silverware to conversation, then the chairman has to decide that they are finished, and that he's got to get on with it.

I began by introducing the committee — calling their names, alternating names of people on the right and left. As I called names, the committee stood up, one by one. On a verbal cue, the whole committee sat down together. Then I introduced the Toastmaster, Isaac Asimov, and handed him the bronze plaque we'd prepared as a memento for the occasion. I had previously given him the plaque for the Guest of Honor, but the plaque for the Toastmaster was a surprise to him. The Good Doctor thanked us, spoke briefly, introduced Will Jenkins (Murray Leinster), and gave *him* his plaque.

Will Jenkins spoke his piece — not long, but interestingly. When he showed signs of coming to the end of his talk, I scribbled a note "plenty of time!" But by then he had started an anecdote designed to lead up to an ending, so I had no chance to get him to talk further.

When Will finished, Isaac took the floor again. He fired off a few jokes and then got down to business: the Hugos. Since the winners are a strictly-kept secret until the last instant, we managed it this way: when he was ready, I passed him a slip of paper with the title of the first category: Best Professional Magazine. Then I put the first Hugo up on the podium, while he read off the category and (from the Program Book) the nominees. He the unfolded the paper to read the winner: *The Magazine of Fantasy & Science Fiction.* To accept the award: Isaac Asimov.

Now, Isaac had never received a Hugo before, and he said as much when he started his talk. I thought that receiving the Hugo for *F&SF* would quiet him. Instead, he Pulled Out All the Stops. He plained at length about how, now that he was no longer writing much science fiction, Hugos were being given out. He said . . . well, read the *Discon Proceedings* for his exact words; enough to say he went on and on about never getting a Hugo, while he passed out Hugos to Dick Lupoff (Best Amateur magazine, *Xero*), Jim Blish on behalf of Philip K. Dick (Best Novel, *The Man in the High Castle*), Fred Pohl on behalf of Jack Vance (Best Short Fiction, "The Dragon Masters") and Don Wollheim on behalf of Roy Krenkel (Best Artist). The last slip of the series was for Best Dramatic Production.

There was a Hugo on the table when Isaac opened the slip and read "No Award." He looked puzzled; obviously there were more Hugos to be awarded, but the categories were exhausted.

I handed him a slip and he read: "Special Award No. 1: P. Schuyler Miller, for The Reference Library." And there I sat with another Hugo in hand.

Another slip of paper. "Special Award No. 2," he read, without looking at the name of the winner.

At this point Isaac paused to speak a few words on the subject of Other People getting Hugos. For the first time during the whole con, I relaxed. I felt like leaning back in my chair and putting my feet on the table; I knew exactly what was going to happen next — and, of course, it did. Isaac finally opened the slip of paper, read it, looked blank, turned away from the audience for a moment, and then turned to me and wailed: "You've ruined my whole bit!!!" What with all the applause, I don't think anybody actually heard him announce the second special award:

"To Isaac Asimov, for putting science into science fiction."

Later, on his way to his hotel room to deposit his loot, Isaac claimed that we had led him on; the change of Toastmaster from Sturgeon to Asimov, the Toastmaster plaque, even the *F&SF* Hugo which he accepted — all these, he said, convinced him that he was not getting a Hugo, and so he could really go to town on the subject.

Yes, the banquet represents the most work of any item on the program. But it can be the most fun . . .

V. THE PROGRAM: SUNDAY EVENING

In the past few years, con committees have chosen to do rather different things with the time immediately following the banquet. One put the costume ball immediately after the banquet — well, allowing time between for folk to change clothes, naturally! Others put the business session there, which at least ensures that the business session will be well attended. Chicon III put Fritz Leiber's lecture, "Fafhrd and Me," immediately after the banquet; it turned out to be the most heavily attended session of that con.

The bit is this: practically *everybody* goes to the banquet. Immediately afterwards, nobody's going to be drifting off to eat, so they're likely to attend whatever program item comes right there. Chicon III, wisely, put that prize program item in this slot. For the Discon, we put in what we thought was our own best item, "What Should a BEM Look Like?"

I think we did right. That session was extremely well attended. With the panelists we had — de Camp, Asimov, Ley, Emsh, Leiber, and Brackett — it couldn't help but be successful as well. This panel can be used as a "for example" to illustrate several points on panel-planning.

For one thing, we arranged with the hotel to set up the speakers' table for panels with the podium at one end, rather than in the middle. This proved to be a distinct advantage: the moderator or chairman of a panel will have all of his panel on only one side of him, so he can take in his whole panel with a single glance, rather than having to look both right and left to see who wants to answer a point just raised.

A second consideration in planning panels: don't have too many, and don't have them too close together. We had four during the con (plus the fanzine art panel, which was mostly a questions-from-the-audience affair.)

Another consideration: get panelists who don't have the same outlook on the subject at hand. With this panel, De Camp, Asimov, and Ley could be expected to approach the topic from pretty strict biological points of view. On the other hand, Fritz Leiber started by saying that an extraterrestrial should be beautiful; Leigh Brackett and Ed Emsh also considered factors other than biological probability in presenting their views.

It was just about the end of this panel that I was hit by a horrible sequence of thoughts: first, though I had invited Seabury Quinn to speak, he hadn't sent me an acceptance for the time finally selected; second, I didn't have the least idea what Quinn looked like, except he was well along in years; and, third, there obviously wasn't time to phone him. I got Joe Sarno, who happened to be willing and available (Yesht bless him) to go to the back of the meeting room and ask "all the elderly men there if they were Seabury Quinn." Luck! The first one asked was the next speaker. There were a few awkward moments: Quinn is nearly blind, and had to be helped to the speakers' table, which was on a low platform. And while I was persuading Bill Evans to introduce him (Bill knows far more about Quinn's writings than I do), Frank Dietz almost got Quinn to begin his speech, and was stopped barely in time.

All went well, however. Quinn spoke briefly, contrasting a fantasy horror story and a science-fiction horror story [*Dr. Faustus* and *RUR*], and did it effectively. He spoke in a very low voice, however, and it was difficult to hear him, in spite of the microphone system. The audience was dead quiet, but I had to go out the entrance doors and quiet a couple of folk who were shouting just outside, including Walter Breen. [This wasn't our first run-in with St. Bushybeard: during registration, Saturday morning, the Hotel convention manager, Mr. van Buren, spotted Breen eating lunch out of a paper bag in the upper lobby, and asked us to ask him to do his paperbag-lunching a little less publically. Bob Pavlat passed the word *that* time.]

After Quinn, some more auction. And after that, starting a few minutes late, came the Business Meeting, which in an excess of wishful thinking I had scheduled for just 30 minutes. At this juncture, things Did Not Go Well.

The Big Heart Award has, for years, been presented at the banquet, along with the Hugos. Furthermore, this year, First Fandom (a club of *old*-timers in fandom) decided to give an award of their own, and hoped to give it at the banquet. Forry Ackerman, who presented the Big Heart award, though unhappy to have the presentation removed from the banquet, took the change in good grace. Don Ford, who was deeply involved in the First Fandom award (though he wasn't the one to make the speech) was unhappy too. In fact, for a while he was furious, declaring that cutting the First Fandom award out of the banquet was a Pretty Chicken Thing; afterward, though, he saw the point — we'll come to it shortly. He was particularly bugged by the fact that, though one of the reasons given for shifting the award was that we were worried about having enough time for everything in the three hours allotted to the banquet, it had turned out the banquet only ran two and a half hours.

As it was, Ackerman made his award speech; the winner was Jimmy Taurasi, who wasn't there to receive it personally. Then Sam Moskowitz rose to make the First Fandom award speech; the winner was E.E. Smith, Ph.D. Sam's speech, though a bit longer than we had planned for, got a tremendous hand for Doc Smith when he came up to get the trophy; in fact, the biggest hand, I think, that anybody got during the whole con.

This points up the other reason we had for keeping the miscellaneous awards out of the banquet. The banquet is to honor the Guest of Honor first, and the Hugo winners second. A response like the one Doc Smith got for this First Fandom award would have put everybody else — including the Guest of Honor — very definitely in second place, and this would have been embarrassing to everyone.

Anyway, the awards were followed by a three minute speech by Janie Lamb in which she gave TAFF (in the person of Ron Ellik) $20 from the NFFF, about which I had been warned, and then a five minute speech on behalf of TAFF by Ellik, about which I hadn't. By this time, the business session still hadn't started, we had a potentially long meeting ahead, and we were running about half an hour late. There was, thank goodness, no other award.

The meeting itself was to be run by Robert's Rules of Order, Revised. The order of business, announced beforehand, was: reports by committees; motions submitted in writing beforehand to the chairman; selection of the site for the 1964 World Science Fiction Convention; and other motions from the floor.

We had two committees to report: a committee formed by a resolution (passed by the Chicon III business meeting) to look into the design of the Hugos; and a committee appointed by the chairman of the Discon, me, to look into the convention rules.

The Hugo committee had, during its deliberations by mail, rather quickly abandoned the idea of changing the rocket-ship design that had become traditional, and had concentrated on providing a replacement source for the trophies themselves, since Ben Jason had retired from making them. The Michigan fans volunteered (thru Howard Devore) to take responsibility for the Hugos in the future, and a resolution to that effect was passed.

The next matter was a bit more complicated. The incorporation of the World Science Fiction Society had been thoroughly discredited some years ago, but nothing has really taken its place, as far as a continuing body of rules went. There is now a continuing corporation, but it is an incorporation of the convention committee only, as explained elsewhere. [Ch. IX, 9.01]

The rules committee, of whom the most active members were Steve Schultheis, Howard Devore, and F. M. Busby, came up with a proposed constitution, which is discussed in Chapter X.

Now, how was the meeting to handle these matters run? Copies of the proposed Constitution had been available at the registration desk; more were distributed at the business meeting. Steve explained why various parts were the way they were, and then it was up to the chairman.

Now, there are lots of people who think that Robert's Rules of Order are sort of a last resort in case of difficulties. Not at all; Robert devised and revised his rules to take care of all kinds of meetings and business sessions. These rules have all kinds of provisions for short-cutting procedural steps, but always with the rights of everybody to be heard on any subject that is pertinent to the discussion at hand carefully safeguarded.

Furthermore, Robert gave the chairman a remarkable lot of powers; for example, the power to refuse to entertain a motion on the grounds that it is frivolous or time-wasting can be used very effectively to shut up compulsive noisemakers. Therefore, we found no reason to run the business meeting by anything other than Robert's Rules of Order, Revised [the 1951 revision, to be exact] since the Rules have all the necessary short-cuts already built in. Too, the chairman has the right and the duty to remind the assembly before him of what motions are appropriate at any time. In this case, a report had been made by a committee. I explained, therefore, that the courses of action open to the meeting were: to debate the report; to refer it to a committee; to implement it by moving the constitution be adopted; or to reject it by voting it down. The remaining possibility — a vote to accept the report of the committee — wouldn't be appropriate.

In the debate that followed, several minor errors were picked up in the printed version of the constitution which had been distributed. These were all amended by general consent — that is, since no one objected to having the corrections made, there was no formality of a vote on them. Both George Raybin and Dave Kyle spoke in favor of the proposed constitution; since it was well known that the two had been on opposite sides of the old incorporation fuss of a few years ago, this helped make up the meeting's mind. When nobody wanted to say anything further, I put the motion — that the constitution be adopted — to a voice vote. It passed handily.

Now, note: it was not necessary to "call the question"; unless the debate is unreasonably drawn out, the chairman lets it continue until there is nobody left who has anything further to say, and then puts the matter to a vote. What helped *that* along was that I kept reminding the meeting that there wasn't an awful lot of time to debate this, and that if things got too drawn out, the matter could be referred to a committee. The biggest thing that allowed a very complex document to be adopted in such a short time was that the matter had been thrashed out in committee beforehand, and that there were written copies of the result available since the beginning of the con for people to think over and digest. I would have liked to call a small meeting some morning before the business meeting for discussion of the constitution with whoever was interested, but I just never got around to it.

Considerable thanks should go to Steve Schultheis, who is the originator of the present constitution. He told me his ideas, I codified them, he made further corrections, and there it was.

The rest of the evening went smoothly, though late. Fred Pohl managed the astounding feat of staying in control of a panel which included John W. Campbell. Then Juanita Coulson, Maggie Thompson, and Ted White answered questions on how to put art work on stencils for mimeographed fanzines; afterward, they gave a demonstration of stencil cutting. The thing that kept the panel from being more successful was simply time; the schedule had slipped back and back (largely because I had underestimated the amount of time for the Business Meeting) until it was so late the audience had begun to dissipate.

VI. LAST SESSION

Monday of a science fiction convention is supposed to be fold-up day, when everybody's busy packing and saying goodbye and starting home early. For *us*, Monday was as well-attended a day of program as any, which goes to show just how far you should trust advice based on previous cons. [Though of course "come early and stay late" has been a growing trend for several years now — F.M. Busby]

Our Monday started with an auction session at 11:30, devoted mainly to spreading the black-and-white art work out among those that wanted it. At 12:00, there was an Edgar Rice Burroughs panel. Alan Howard was moderator; the participants included Dick Lupoff, Sam Moskowitz, L. Sprague de Camp, and Alan Howard. In a way, it was a continuation of a panel with many of the same participants that cut off for lack of time at the last Lunacon. Considering the strong feelings that Burroughs arouses, it is surprising that things did go as smoothly as they did, even tho someone innocently asked, "Is it true that Burroughs was a racist?" [Not "innocently"; I did it a'purpose.] Sprague saved the reputation of the wizard of Tarzana on that one, by explaining that Burroughs was no more, and perhaps less, racially tilted than other writers of his time.

The next item on the program was one that had been invented specifically for Tony Boucher to moderate. The subject: Life with a Stf Writer. The participants: a choice selection of wives; Carol Pohl and Edna Budrys, wives of combination editors-and-writers; Barbara Silverberg, wife of a writer; Carol Emshwiller, wife of an artist, and a writer herself. Well. Boucher couldn't make it to the Discon, so I arranged to Ted Cogswell to take the panel instead. Unfortunately, when 1:00 PM came, Cogswell couldn't be found. There was a moment of indecision; here were these lovely wives, without a chairman to run their panel. But no more than a moment, before I dashed to the microphone (before anybody else could) and announced that I would run the panel.

It was fun. The basic theme was, "What should a young girl expect to have to put up with from a writer (or editor, or artist) husband?" The questions ran from "How do you know he's working?" on to "Are you allowed to dust his typewriter or paintbrushes?" After I ran out of questions, I let the audience ask theirs, limiting the questions to those from ladies in the audience. Finally it was over; too soon, but after all the fuss I'd made about *other* people running on time... Anyway, I kissed each of the wives, gave the husbands a bottle of Hudson's Bay scotch to share, and it was over. Being chairman is sometimes a cruelly demanding chore. . . .

There was an intermission, with another short bit of auction . . .

Oh yes, the reason that conventions seem to spend so much time on auction. It is that chairmen and program planners usually underestimate the amount of time the auction will require, so that every extra squitch of time is turned over to the auctioneers. The best cures: (1) limit the auction material, and (2) allow plenty of time for the scheduled auction period.

Hal Clement and P. Schuyler Miller were next, with a topic that Hal had thought up: "Is the Science Fiction Story a Mental Exercise, Like the Detective Story?" Hal took the affirmative, Schy the contrary. They came to no definite conclusion, but they (and the audience, who joined the discussion) had fun trying.

The skit, whose principal instigators were Judy Merril, Fritz Leiber, and Gordon Dickson, wasn't ready yet. The skit was still collecting props; white lab coats, bottles, a table lamp, signs. For a while the hotel was overrun with a sort of stefnistic scavenger hunt. Anyway, the schedule was switched; the skit was postponed, and the item rather ambiguously titled "The Fourth Convention" went on next.

This was based on a concept I invented some years ago, in an article in SPHERE, that there are really three conventions going on at once: a convention of pro authors, a convention of stf readers, and a convention of fans, and the three cons operate pretty much independently of each other. Ted Sturgeon used the idea in his Chicon III speech. Shortly after the Discon committee got to work on preparation, we realized that there are not three but *four* different cons. The fourth is the one the con committee sees — the behind-the-scenes work. So, for "The Fourth Convention," the panel consisted of all the members of past con committees that were attending the Discon, from NYCon I on to the Discon itself.

It was quite a crowd. There was a dismaying tendency for the old con committee members to fall off the speakers' platform; as one was picking herself up after tripping, Dave Kyle (of NYCon II fame) remarked, with a sad shake of his head: "There goes a former con committee chairman. See what it does to us . . . ?"

The group discussed past cons briefly. Then de Camp summed up the advice for future cons neatly: expect that everything will take twice as long and cost twice as much as you had planned, and be sure the chairman is in reasonably robust health. Dave Kyle said that the present custom of buying membership in a con well in advance of the con date was a life-saver for the con treasuries; Will Sykora apologized (or was it Sam Moskowitz?) for the famous exclusion act at NYCon I and explained that it was chiefly because the con committee were inexperienced and afraid something would go wrong, politically, if they *didn't* exclude. And finally Ben Stark, a chairman of the Pacificon II, was dragged bodily up to the platform by Evans and de Camp and presented with the World Science Fiction Society gavel and a promise of a check for $300 from the Discon treasury.

The skit came next; though poorly heard (as all such things are, because of the difficulty of getting microphones to cover the actors' lines), it was fun.

And suddenly the skit was over. The Discon was ended, and the members, fans, pros, readers or what you will, were beginning to drift away. Not so the con committee; it wasn't until Tuesday noon that we had the last of our stuff packed away. And again, it was our very good fortune that we had assistance, notably Ron Ellik and his group, to help us with the packing and moving of stuff from the convention suite down to our automobiles. (Of course, Ellik *did* mistakenly pack the con-committee correspondence file and cart it off to Los Angeles.)

The aftermath — beyond Tuesday — took months of rather leisurely work to finish off. Bob Pavlat took the address list and the left-over program books and give-away material, and mailed a set out to each con member who didn't attend. Bill Evans had the finances to complete and the bills to pay. Dick Eney had the *Proceedings* to edit [Ahahahahaha! — RE] I have been writing this report.

A minor point — perhaps even one that is so obvious it should not be covered here — is nonetheless a very necessary extra. You should assign one member of your committee the task of saying "Thank you." This job is especially good if you have a shut-in committee member, a housewife who can't spend too much time at committee meetings, etc. Every contributor of auction material, every person who accepts a program commitment, etc., should receive a letter of acknowledgment with a prominent, explicit "thank you" in it somewhere. It does not matter if they get more than one expression of thanks. But it might very well matter, the next time they are asked for their assistance and co-operation, if their last efforts on behalf of out conventions were apparently overlooked.

And meanwhile, in Berkeley and London, other conventions are being organized, programs are being lined up, plans are being laid for the banquet and ball, and the next World Science Fiction Conventions begin to take form. It'll be fun to watch *this* one from the sidelines.

VII. ACCESSORY ORGANIZATIONS

7.01: The first thing that you, as a potential con committee member, must realize when considering the various Worthy Organizations and Causes in fandom is that the responsibility of a con committee is to put on a con; all other Worthy Causes get taken care of on an "if there's extra time and money" basis, or not at all. It is well to remember that the World Science Fiction Society is the closest thing there is to a country-wide science fiction (and fantasy) organization. The Society, together with the convention committee which does the actual running of the con, is the senior organization in the field, and I suspect that a good part of its success is because the Society has such limited objectives: to have a convention, to award Hugos, and to select a site for the next year's convention. The Society membership is not limited to "fans"; a substantial part of the membership consists of readers and writers of science fiction.

7.02: Now, the N3F (the National Fantasy Fan Federation) is an old and well-known fan organization. In its more enthusiastic moments, it has tried to speak for "all fandom." However, even if it had succeeded, the N3F doesn't and can't represent the writers and the non-fan readers of science fiction.

Through the years, the N3F and the successive con committees have reached sort of a tacit agreement about their relationship. The N3F, for its part, provides the supplies and the management (including supervision) of a hospitality room — usually a small suite or a small meeting room. This room provides coffee and cookies and the like for con members, particularly the younger ones, who have time on their hands during the con, especially late in the evening while the older folk are off at more or less private parties.

The con committee's contribution has varied from convention to convention. While sometimes the con committee has done nothing but accept the services provided by the N3F (for the hospitality room does provide the committee a service by keeping the younger, newer con attendees out of trouble), the more usual arrangement is for the con committee to provide the room space. There are several ways this can be done. One, used by the Discon, is for the committee to assign to the N3F one of the complimentary rooms provided by the hotel. Another method, used by Chicon III, is for the committee to let the N3F engage a room on their own hook and pay for it, as well as for the food used, and then donate to the N3F a sum of money equal to the whole expenditure. Some con committees have also given the N3F enough money to reimburse the Federation even for the cost of the food & drink given out in the hospitality room.

The principal difficulty with the first method, giving the N3F a room outright, is that arranging for the room is extra work for the con committee; we had to spend several hours untangling the general confusion until the N3F was finally settled into a room, and then we almost had to pay for an extra room they moved into by mistake. In retrospect, it would have been better for us to have asked the N3F to reserve a room on their own, with no other commitment but that we'd give them a donation equal to the cost of the room, *if* we found we could afford it. (In our case, we could have.)

Although the N3F room does the con a service, it provides a few potential headaches too. If the N3F-provided hostesses have a firm hand and a no-nonsense attitude, there's no problem. However, it is possible for the room to become an overnight sleeping place for fans too cheap to hire a room of their own, and it is possible for the room to become the scene of a heavy drinking party. Neither of these is the Hospitality Room designed to be, and if either of these possibilities develops, the con committee will have to step in, ready to eject sleepers, confiscate drinks, or even — if things get incredibly out of hand — close down the room. In the past, the N3F hostesses have always been able to keep things under control, though sometimes just barely.

As a rule, the N3F will seek as much help with the Hospitality Room as they can get from the committee, in the form of food-buying, room-supervising, and the like. And, as a rule, each con committee will figure out (on the basis of their own individual situation), just what help they *can* provide in the way of help, and provide that much. To me, the most important point is that the N3F, not the con committee, is responsible for providing hostesses to keep the room under reasonable control. Emergency help is another matter; the knowledge that the con committee are ready to help the hostesses if things start coming apart at the seams is at least a moral assist.

In the case of the N3F and the Discon, the emergency help that was called for was given *by* the N3F *to* the con committee [Described in the Appendix.] In that sticky situation, the con committee never had a moment's worry over the matter; everything was handled neatly by the N3Fers.

Although the N3F is subject to internal feuds, a strong defensive reaction to intentional and unmeant criticism, and a tendency to charge off in several different directions at once, it is a well-established and stable organization. It has been in existence since 1941; it has a big enough treasury and enough expertise to carry out what it sets out to do, within reason. The relationship between the con committees and the N3F, therefore, has been one of mutual assistance rather than dependance. A hard-pressed con committee can call on, and get, help from the N3F; a particularly strong con committee can offer substantial assistance to the N3F during the con.

7.03: TAFF (the Trans-Atlantic Fan Fund . . . what, you knew?) and other funds like it are another matter entirely. These funds supply an interesting visitor from Europe from time to time — which visitor, let's face it, is interesting primarily to fanzine fans. The convention, on the other hand, is usually asked for a substantial donation to the fund. In addition, some (but not all) conventions visited by TAFF representatives have provided the hotel room at the convention at con expense.

It is my feeling, first, that the convention should commit itself to provide such funds with nothing at all until the convention books have been pretty well settled, and, second, that the donation should be only a token one. There is general agreement in the Discon Committee on the first point; it is foolish for a con committee to give away money until they are sure they have it. There is substantial disagreement on the second point. *I* feel that TAFF is of interest only to the fanzine-type fans at the convention, and that they should be the support, not the convention. If the fans are not interested enough to support TAFF directly, they should not find themselves supporting it indirectly. On the other hand, Dick Eney feels that there isn't as much of a Great Gulf Fixed between fanzine fans, convention fans, readers, and pros as some people would make out; that conventions are an appropriate time, if any time is, to emphasise fans' common interest and fandom's international character; and that if convention committees are unable to figure out how people like Ethel Lindsay, Wally Weber, Art Thomson, or Terry Carr — to go no further into the past — could make the convention more enjoyable, they simply aren't being imaginative enough.

7.04: Project Art Show, on the other hand, is an attraction, and benefits all con members in immediately obvious ways. If the convention could insure its continued existence merely by donating money, it would certainly be worth it. However, the amateur art show, for its continued successful existence, needs manpower more than it needs money.

This is the one thing that hardly any con committee can afford to provide. The reason, as we've hinted earlier, is that running a successful convention — that is, the main events: the ball, the banquet, the program itself, and the necessary preparations like awards, auction material, and program books — will take about all the willing-and-responsible manpower that is available in one city. The art show, therefore, *must* depend on out-of-town help for everything except having a local fan receive artwork mailed in advance. Furthermore, Project Art Show by its very nature needs a continuing organization to keep it going effectively, and this a con committee, by nature, is not. All in all, then, the committee can best help this valuable adjunct to the convention by providing — at committee expense, if the hotel isn't being generous — a good display room for the art work. (At Discon, the room was 40 feet by 50, though we didn't fill it to the brim.) Beyond that, plus a financial shot in the arm if needed, and plenty of publicity in the progress reports and the program book, there just isn't that much a convention committee *can* do to help.

7.05: One thing the convention committee will have to watch out for with the accessory activities, and that is fund raising. What with the auction, which is run for the benefit of the convention treasury, and the various new and used book sellers, the convention attendee faces a lot of demands for his money. Too much of this thing will mar the convention. An unfortunate example of this was the Auction Bloch — a nice novelty idea, and a good money-maker for TAFF when it first started — but an idea which outlived its interest quickly, until it became a time-taking drag before Chicon III finally killed it.

As a matter of principle, the convention committee should never stand in the way of a general feeling among fans that something or other should be allowed to die for lack of interest.

7.06: From time to time, someone will come up with a good-looking idea of one sort or another for some new accessory activity of the convention. Convention committees must watch these with extreme care, not only for their own sake, but also for the sake of the convention committees which will follow.

A factor which many convention-goers haven't fully appreciated is that the convention committee is *not* a continuing body. One convention cannot — must not — commit the next convention to something it may not want to get involved with. For example, take Harriet Kolchak's Neo Fund, a scheme for helping out young fans who find themselves without sufficient funds at a convention. Now, the problem of the unfunded fan is one that turns up from time to time. And convention committees have used their own judgement on who to give a few dollars to and who to send to the nearest Travelers' Aid. (Of course, someone who makes a career of "losing his wallet" at conventions will be lots more likely to be sent to Travelers' Aid.) At first glance, an organization to take care of such problems might look like a Good Thing for convention committees. How*ever*, if such an organization did get started with convention committee backing, and then later, for one reason or another, suddenly failed, the next convention committee would find itself stuck with the implied obligation to take care of the fundless ones. Therefore, the Discon committee declined the request of the Neo Fund for program time to announce its aims, but instead insisted that the Neo Fund operate as a sort of accessory to the N3F room, provided the N3F had no objection. [Harriet Kolchak was one of the N3F hostesses at Discon.]

7.07: In the same way, convention committees must be wary about getting involved with seers of flying saucers, and like fauna. It isn't that belief in airborne crockery is objectionable *per se*, but that flying saucer fans enormously outnumber the science fiction readers, authors, and fans who now form the bulk of Worldcon membership, and it would be awfully easy for us to get swamped. However, groups of reasonable size, who are closely allied with science fiction and fantasy, have long had meetings within the framework of a Worldcon — usually in the mornings, when all ~~sensible~~ other folk are still recovering from the parties of the night before. These organizations range in size from the Burroughs Bibliophiles through the Hyborian Legion, FAPA, SAPS, and the Dorcas Bagby Society on down (apt direction!) to The Cult. The only real problem with these groups is getting them to state their need for a meeting room well in advance of the con, so announcement can be made in the program book and a room can be reserved for them at the appropriate time.

7.08: Parties? Now's the time to lay one misconception to rest. The truth of the matter is that parties at science fiction conventions are definitely *not* as noisy as the parties at other types of conventions . . . nearly, but definitely not quite. You must understand that the management of a hotel that has much convention business *expects* that they will have to quiet down a dozen or so parties during the course of a convention weekend. If things get too much out of hand, the con committee may be asked to help with an extremely noisy affair or two, but this degree of trouble is very rare. The only festivities that make for really significant trouble is the costume ball. At the SoLACon, one of the contestants, garbed as a priest of an arcane religion and wearing sackcloth, ashes, and a smoke pot, went out into Pershing Square after the ball and preached. When the crowd grew large, the fan returned to the hotel, followed by a good part of his new congregation. Then the people in the hotel, still in costume, looked out of the windows to see what was going on. When the motorists in the streets below stopped to goggle, the police dropped in to ask — in a nice way — for the con to please stop whatever it was that they were doing. (The hotel detective at this point was laughing so hard he wasn't any help to *any*body. Again, at Chicon III, a group of Catholic Youth in the hotel for a convention off their own wandered into the costume ball in such numbers that the room was too crowded for a proper costume parade. The Discon was strongly advised by the hotel management to have a uniformed guard, particularly since there was another convention at the hotel at the same time. We are very glad we did. The Other Convention turned out to be a high school fraternity . . .

VIII. MORE AFTERMATH: MONEY & THE PROCEEDINGS

8.01 To begin with, let's look at the final financial report of the Discon.

INCOME:

Donation from Chicon III	374.16
Memberships & Fees	2194.00
Banquet sales	2203.25
Auction sales	1180.52
Ads in Progress Reports & Program book	285.50
GROSS INCOME	$6237.43

EXPENSES:

Printing & paper	288.18
Engertainment of Guest of Honor	182.88
Legal services	245.00
Insurance	71.32
Sales tax	46.71
Cost & commissions on auction material	445.45
Banquet costs (442 covers)	2253.52
Hugos	306.58
Telephone	77.80
Costume ball	76.61
Band	380.00
Projector rental	74.00
Registration & meeting	178.99
Office expenses	56.11
Postage	103.26
Donation to Trans-Atlantic Fan Fund	100.00
Taxes on revenues, etc.	150.00
Reserved for Final Progress Report	40.00
Reserved for printing of *Proceedings*	700.00
To PacifiCon II	440.02
GROSS EXPENSES	$6237.43

Discon had about 600 registrants; Chicon III, about 600; Seacon, about 300. But Chicon estimates about 100 non-paying attendees, while we had a dozen or so at our gathering.

8.02 Notes are now in order. The largest single item is always the banquet. Ideally, the income from the banquet and the outgo should be very nearly equal. (The price of a hotel banquet is always so high that you'd be ill advised to try and make a profit; too much chance of killing the banquet altogether.) Since this *is* such a large item, however, it's easy to see how a small percentage error in a guarantee of tickets to a hotel can ruin a convention, as happened in New York. The next largest item is *usually* printing and related costs; the Discon achieved its low cost here by doing all the progress reports and the program book on the convention chairman's Ancient and

Venerable Multilith, so that the costs cited are for negatives, plates, and paper alone. More typical figures are those for Chicon III (about $800) and Seacon (about $500). Detroit obtained some savings by the use of a mimeographed first Progress Report.

Another highly variable item is the cost of the band. All you can do, as a general thing, is either to have a band or else not. If you do have one, the cost is set by the local Musicians' Union. Another significant figure: the total turnover of money ranges from about $3,400 to $6,500; this is why a competent, reliable, and unquestionably honest treasurer is a m*u*s*t. This amount of money practically dictates another expense, which should be expected to settle down at about $150 a year: the legal expenses. This represents the amount of work performed by the convention's lawyer, in keeping the con committee out of trouble.

8.03 Now, Seattle donated about $1,025 to various Worthy Causes. Chicon III began a new tradition, which the Discon and — hopefully — Pacificon II are continuing, of publishing a *Proceedings* of the convention. This publication seems to be an ideal disposition of excess money from the convention; first, it benefits the whole membership of the convention, and second, it is an expense which can be changed from year to year to fit the amount of money available, simply by varying the amount over and above membership fee that members will be charged.

In its original concept, the *Proceedings* would be a continuing, yearly volume. *The Proceedings: Chicon III* was actually title number two in a series; volume one is a pictorial and verbal recap of all previous worldcons — a book that has already been under research for three years and is now slowly evolving into manuscript form.

The Proceedings: Discon becomes number three in a series, with number one still a good distance in the future.

For *The Proceedings: Chicon III*, considerable advance work was done to eliminate as many of the potential cost factors as were possible to foresee. It is strongly recommended that your committee, if you wish to see the series continue, also attempt to economize in similar fashion.

For instance, aside from the costs of actual physical manufacture, the single most expensive item is obtaining a transcription of the convention as recorded. In this case, Chicago asked every single program member, wherever possible, to provide a manuscript version of their portion of the program. This resulted in a very significant saving. All that was necessary was to compare the manuscript with the transcription and mark in any deviations from the prepared lecture. Transcribing such a massive thing as thirteen to eighteen hours of continuous lecture is no job for an amateur. Consequently, the services of a professional transcriber are necessary for filling in around the manuscript portions. As in all professions, rates are high when compared with the usual fan publication costs.

Photographs are also an expensive item. To cover most events, Chicago arranged for two photographers, loaded with many rolls of black and white film, to cover the entire convention. Their photographs were augmented with pictures taken by other fans to produce the results you saw last year. Discon failed to make such arrangements [It was another of those Things We Just Didn't Think Of.] but luckily managed to contact J. K. Klein, who filled in the pages single handed. The use of black-and-white film is very important, as the conversion from color to black-and-white for reproduction is pretty expensive. Of course, to print the *Proceedings* with color pages would be out of the question; color runs over $100 a single page. The use of photographs in the *Proceedings*, obviously, is to provide a pictorial record as well as a verbal record, and also to break up the monotony of continuous pages of text.

Since, as we've said before, convention committees are not continuing bodies, and the production of the *Proceedings* entails almost one additional year's work after the convention, the committee decided to turn the production of the series over to Advent: Publishers, rather than attempting to hold the committee together for another year. Advent: handles the composition, the manufacture, and the distribution of the *Proceedings* (and in the test cases of Chicago and Washington has agreed to underwrite any additional costs necessary over a basic minimum) at actual cost.

Initially, with *The Proceedings: Chicon III,* the cost estimates were considerably off. The book was offered to all qualified takers at a price of 50¢ per copy. The actual cost to manufacture the book, without counting postage and wrappings, ran to some 80+¢ per copy. About $350+ was contributed by Advent: to make the book an actuality, with the hope of recovering this outlay through over-the-counter sales. The Discon, aware of these problems, voted to raise the initial allocation for the manufacture of *The Proceedings: Discon* and to raise the initial price to $1 per copy (for the membership, that is, and within a given time period). This new price of $1 per copy, including wrapping and postage, insures that the members are getting their copies at just under actual manufacture costs.

At this writing, negotiations with Berkeley are stalled, but investigations of the practicability of producing *The Proceedings: Pacificon II* are still going on. Watch the news magazines. Even if actual production isn't possible, three consecutive convention committees agree that it's desirable, and seriously suggest your continuation of the series.

IX. INSURANCE AND OTHER PRECAUTIONS

We've already told you about our Armed, Uniformed Guard. We also had some other precautions, no less helpful for our peace of mind, but less gaudy and conspicuous.

9.01 For one thing, the 21st World Science Fiction Convention, Inc., *was* inc. That is to say, the Chicon III convention committee retained a lawyer, who did the necessary things to form the World Science Fiction Convention, Incorporated, a non-profit corporation organized under the laws of the State of Illinois.

The corporation is essentially the convention committee, and exists for their protection. It has no effect on the general membership of the convention at all.

The corporation charter is quite broad; the corporation is organized for the purpose of putting on conventions, and such other activities as the board of directors may decide. The first board of directors were the Chicon III committee, and, originally, the corporation was to last only until sometime in January 1964, to cover just Chicon III and the Discon. After Chicon III, the then board of directors elected the Discon committee to be their successors and resigned. After an agreement was reached between the Pacificon II and the Discon committees, the legal counsel of the corporation (who is the only part of the corporation who *has* to be in Illinois) was instructed to have the corporation charter amended to last to perpetuity. (He offered to try and amend the charter to last *beyond* perpetuity if we wanted, and then make it a test case before the courts, but . . .) Then, after the Discon, the Discon Committee elected the Pacificon II Committee to be the new board of directors, effective the 1st of January 1964, and resigned ourselves, effective the same date.

It is to be expected that, when the convention is held outside of the United States, that instead of passing the incorporation on to the foreign convention committee (which would hand them a bushel of tricky problems with foreign-corporation laws) the most recent U.S. con committee will remain as a board of directors without duties, and the Corporation will become inactive until some following U.S. convention takes it up. Why not just let it lapse? Well, the original formation of a corporation costs several hundred dollars to accomplish. While it can be dissolved at any time, that will cost another hundred-odd dollars. Thus, once the corporation is formed, it's wiser to keep it as long as there appears to be any future need for it.

What is this need? The very important necessity of keeping the finances of committee members and convention separate: not only to avoid bankrupting the committee if a con goes broke, but also to regularize tax returns and the like.

9.02 As previously mentioned, there is a grapevine of information flowing freely from hotel to hotel, regardless of affiliation, concerning the minutest details of the operations of science fiction conventions. A similar dossier most likely exists in the convention bureaus, from city to city. And you can rest assured Uncle Sam is watching you too, if you're the type that finds that a restful thought. The local sales tax situation within the District of Columbia was covered under the heading "The Auction." You will probably find your committee faced with a similar situation. Check this out ahead of time so you will not have to pay these taxes out of your own pockets.

A special form (currently color-coded as the "blue" form) is provided by the Bureau of Internal Revenue to cover the operation of your convention for the period of one year. Your convention *is taxable.* Don't wait for the Federal boys to inform you of this fact; pay the taxes before you pass on the balance of cash to the next committee in line.

9.03 And yes, we *did* have insurance, actually and literally; a $300,000/500,000 personal liability policy, protecting the convention in case we got sued as a result of an accident or something. (In passing, I strongly feel that the TAFF administrator would do well to protect himself by taking out a substantial accident insurance policy on each TAFF winner; the repercussions if a TAFFer were killed, say in an auto accident, in the host country would be very painful indeed. *He* might be too courteous to complain, but think of the other fans)

Now, it just might be impossible for a particular convention to obtain this personal liability policy, as underwriting policies differ from location to location, as do requirements for hotel insurance. In Chicago, no company would give coverage, not even the fabled Lloyd's of London. In all cases, the refusal was made because the convention would be held in a hotel (the Pick-Congress) which was already insured and liable for any possible incident. The issuance of such a policy would be compounding the coverage, and no company will underwrite a policy that could result in double payment for one incident.

9.04 Now, the most unpleasant type of insurance of all; protection against known troublemakers. Going by past experiences, we can expect that these, though they will represent a real worry to the con committee, will be rare. And, since a good part of the convention membership are steady con goers, word quickly gets around on the routine nuisances.

A very real, though thank ghod rare, risk remains: someone who preys in one way or another on the younger con members — teenagers and even younger. There are three possible solutions. The Discon committee seriously considered writing to one Problem and pointing out that we were aware what was up, and that the hotel staff was too. The second would be to persuade the hotel management to decline to rent a room to someone named by the committee. The third solution is one for which there is a long-standing precedent; simply bar the individual from the convention meetings.

None of these solutions are sure-fire and all may Plunge All Fandom Into War. The third technique will certainly lead to a long and bitter fight unless the con membership is virtually unanimous in wanting to keep out the objectionable one; if the fellow has friends among the Loud People, you can expect a campaign of vilification to be launched against you automatically. The second technique might work if the hotel management is cooperative, but is chancy; it *might* panic them. The first method may be the best; even if the chap shows up, the warning will probably slow him down a bit. For the prevention of slander, it would be best to seek legal advice before taking any of these actions.

If you *do* have to un-invite someone, remember; the members of past con committees will support your action, and the members of future con committees will be grateful for taking care of what might have been their problem instead. And when do you *have* to? When you find out about the risk, if you're wise. If it comes out at the inquest that you knew of the offender's behaviour and *didn't* bar him, the judge will throw away the key after he locks you up.

In our case, quite frankly, we wish we had sent the letter of un-invitation as an official action. Not for our own sakes, since the Discon did not (as far as we know) have any trouble, but because such a letter would have made the task of our successors that much easier when they had to deal with the problem we avoided.

9.05 One other thing that could cause you considerable embarrassment and unforseen expenditure would be overlooking the local labor union situation. The operation of the different locals, from city to city, allows a wide variety of freedom in one area while imposing seemingly unnecessary or frivolous restrictions in others. In one city, you may not be allowed to turn on a microphone at the podium, but you can operate your own movie projector. In other cities, you may have to provide a union operator for a slide projector, or summon a union electrician to replace a burned-out bulb. And an innocent (or indignant) act on your part could — stretching the point to the extreme — cause a walkout of all the bellhops, the elevator operators, the waiters, the bartenders, the cooks . . .

You can imagine for yourself the consequences for your committee.

X. THE CONSTITUTION AND BYLAWS

— THE WORLD SCIENCE FICTION SOCIETY.

Ever since Anna Sinclaire Moffatt's wildly cheered ruling, "This is the business meeting of the XVI World Science Fiction Convention, and not that of the World Science Fiction Society, Incorporated," an unresolved question has been: are the World Science Fiction Conventions a continuing body, or what? South Gate renounced the incorporation; so did the Detention. By

Pittcon, the corporation was a dead issue. The question of continuity remained: is one convention bound by the rules and precedents of those earlier? Certainly, the rotation plan (which predated the incorporation) continued to function — but more or less by default, since no convention chairman had occasion to rule on the matter. At Pittcon, a committee was formed to study standardizations of the Hugo categories; at Pittcon, a resolution was passed standardizing the *form* of the trophies themselves on the model developed by Ben Jason. At Seacon, a set of rules were adopted to govern the Hugo categories and voting procedures in the future. But — need these rules be followed? The Chicon III committee felt not, but did not make an issue of it; the Discon I committee, on the other hand, felt that the rules and resolutions did constitute a continuing body of rules, and did their best to follow them. But the question of continuity was still unresolved.

At the Chicon III, however, a committee to study the design of the Hugos was formed, the membership appointed by me. During the following year, I formed a second committee, partly out of the first, consisting of myself, Howard Devore, & Steve Schultheis, to study the whole question of continuity and of codification of the mixture of traditions and ancient resolutions that the conventions were operating under. The result was a new constitution and bylaws, based on suggestions by Schultheis and Devore. The final wording was mine, but the ideas are largely Schultheis's. It was submitted to the business meeting of the Discon I and passed there. The constitution and bylaws begin:

1.01 The World Science Fiction Society is an unincorporated literary society whose functions are: to choose the recipients of the annual Science Fiction Achievement Awards, known as the Hugos; to choose the location for the annual World Science Fiction Convention; and to attend the annual World Science Fiction Convention.

1.02 The membership of the World Science Fiction Society at any time consists of all those who have paid membership dues to the then current convention committee.

1.03 The management and responsibility for all phases of the annual World Science Fiction Convention lies entirely with the convention committee, which acts in its own name, not that of the society. The convention committee which puts on the convention is, of course, the committee whose bid for selection of its location is accepted by the annual meeting of the society.

These sections, then, establish that there is an organization — an unincorporated body — called the World Science Fiction Society, which is separate and distinct from the convention committee of the moment. Whether this revives the formerly incorporated Society, or establishes the Society anew after a hiatus of several years, is immaterial; the constitution does state that there is a body, and that it is separate from the con committee.

The reasons for non-incorporation of the Society are several. After the WSFS *Inc.* fiasco of several years ago, fandom wasn't about to have at *that* mess again. Further, incorporation would be expensive to begin and tedious to continue. So, instead, the Society was defined in such a way as to make incorporation totally unnecessary: the Society's *only* functions are to choose the Hugo winners (but not to manufacture the Hugos), to choose the next convention site and attend the convention (but not to manage the convention). *All* financial details were left in the hands of the convention committee; the constitution exerts very little control on the committee — in most areas, none at all.

Section 1.02 is merely definition of the Society membership. Note that the Society has no officers listed, here or elsewhere, since the convention committee provides the presiding officer for the business meeting. And the Society and the con committee are separate bodies; remember that.

The next sections of the constitution and bylaws cover the annual awards:

2.01 The selection of the annual Hugos and the categories for which awards will be made are as follows:

2.02 Best Novel: A science fiction or fantasy novel appearing for the first time as a hard cover book, *or* appearing for the first time as a soft cover book, magazine serial, or complete novel, during the previous calendar year. Previous winners are not eligible, nor shall a story be eligible more than twice. Publication date, or cover date in the case of a dated magazine, shall take precedence over copyright date. At least one installment of a serial shall have been published in the eligible year.

Some explanation before we get any further: these rules (with exceptions noted as we get to them) are essentially the same as those passed at Seattle. As I interpret these rules, a Novel is eligible twice if it appears as a serial and as a hard cover book (unless it wins the first time), or as a paperback and a hard cover book, but is eligible only once if it appears as a serial and as a paperback. The terms "complete novel, or "novel," "science fiction," and "fantasy" are not further defined; it is assumed that convention committees can be trusted to decide what is and what isn't, even if they'd be hard put to come up with written definitions. By implication, anything that occupies a whole hard-cover or soft-cover book, or which is serialized, and otherwise fits the rules, is a Novel. However, anything which otherwise fits the rules and which is a "complete novel" is covered just as well. This, unfortunately, leaves the boundary line between the Novel and a "story of less than novel length" undefined; if anyone comes up with a good distinction, I'd like to see it incorporated in the rules; until then, the convention committee is pretty well on its own in putting things into the proper places.

2.03 Best Short Fiction: A science fiction or fantasy story of less than novel length published for the first time in a magazine, *or* appearing for the first time in a collection or anthology, during the previous calendar year. Previous winners are not eligible, nor shall a story be eligible more than twice. Publication date, or cover date in the case of a dated magazine, shall take precedence over copyright date. Individual stories appearing together as a series are eligible only as individual stories, and are not eligible taken together under the title of the series.

Probably the most difficult point in these rules is the question of what is the difference between a Novel and a piece of Short Fiction, particularly since this award has, for the past two years, been won by stories of considerable length.

The use of publication date or cover date is largely a matter of convenience and consistency; in many cases, the copyright date may be in error by several months in separating what is generally available in one year from what is generally available in the next.

And, as in any body of rules, these too are a compilation of clarifications of disputed situations from the past. The award of a Hugo to a series of stories, instead of to a specifically named member of the series was such a disputed point; the present rule definitely puts all shorter fiction on a more equal footing, competing *as individual stories.*

Whether a collection of stories, however, rates as a Novel is a question which some future convention committee will have to wrestle with — I would say that it would depend on how well-connected the stories were. The Pacificon II, for instance, decided that the hardcover book *Savage Pellucidar* was a collection, not a novel, so placed the shorter story "Savage Pellucidar," which was but a part of the hard cover book, into the

"Shorter Fiction" category — and this seems to be an altogether sensible decision.

The term "previous winners," incidentally, does *not* refer to the authors, but to the stories; "Previous winners are not eligible" means that a story — Novel or Shorter Fiction — having won a Hugo is not eligible for another on reappearance.

2.04 Best Dramatic Production. Any production, single or series, directly related to science fiction or fantasy, in the fields of radio, television, stage, or screen, which has been publicly presented for the first time in its present form during the previous calendar year. In the case of individual programs presented as a series, the separate programs shall be individually eligible, but the entire year's production taken as a whole under the title of the series shall not be eligible.

The point of prohibiting awards for a series was to put an individual TV program on an equal footing with other single performances — otherwise, a TV series, being a continuing thing, had an insuperable advantage over a movie or a play.

Since the rule, two conventions have had "No Award" for the Dramatic Production, which leads to the question — had not the category best be cancelled outright, thus making a Dramatic Presentation able to get a Special Award? Basically, as stated in 1.01 above, the World Science Fiction Society is a *literary* society, not a TV-watching club, and the "No Awards" of recent years seem to bear this out.

2.05 Best Professional Artist: A professional artist whose work was presented in some form in the science fiction or fantasy field during the previous calendar year.

2.06 Best Professional Magazine: Any magazine devoted primarily to science fiction or fantasy,

which has published four or more issues, at least one issue appearing in the previous calendar year.

This one would be better worded "Any *professional* magazine...," and such a change should be made the next time the Constitution and Bylaws are rewritten. However, 2.06 is reasonably clear as it stands — I'm just nitpicking.

2.07 Best Amateur Magazine: Any generally available non-professional magazine devoted to science fiction, fantasy, or related subjects, which has published four or more issues, at least one issue appearing in the previous calendar year.

Although "non-professional" and "generally available" are not defined, I think the terms are well enough understood to be clear. The point of "generally available" is to exclude those magazines available only to members of an amateur press association — to limit consideration to magazines available for subscription, letter of comment, or other means accessible to all.

2.08 Special Award. A Special Award shall be given only when, in the opinion of the convention committee, recognition should be given to either a professional or fan for a special contribution to the field not covered by the annual awards. They shall be identical to the regular Hugos *except* that the plate shall also include the words "Special Award." It must be understood that no convention committee is obligated to give this award, and not only can but should resist pressure for an award thought unmerited. Since the achievements contemplated under this provision are non-competitive, Special Awards shall not be voted on by the Society membership.

2.09 Additional Awards: The name and design of the Hugos shall be restricted to the awards listed

above, and shall not be extended to any additional awards.

At this point we come to a point made controversial by the Pacificon II award to the Best Book Publisher. Sections 2.08 and 2.09 were originally worded by the study group which reported to the Seacon, were followed by Chicon III and Discon, and the sections were confirmed , without change, by the Discon business meeting. In brief, they serve to restrict the name and design of the Hugo rocket ship to those categories, and only those categories, named in 2.02 through 2.07, plus an additional non-competitive category which is distinguished by the words "Special Award." The purpose of all this is to avoid proliferation of Hugo awards until the award becomes meaningless — and this restriction has *not* been challenged at any business meeting.

Now, the Pacificon II chose to award a Hugo to the Best Book Publisher. As a Special Award, well and good. Had they desired the membership's opinion on the matter of who *was* the best book publisher, they could have asked them, "In order that the committee can better make up its mind who *is* the Best Book Publisher, would you indicate your own feeling . . . ?" A subterfuge, admittedly, but I believe it would've been far better than an outright violation of the rules. On the other hand, the Pacificon II committee could have introduced a motion at the Discon business meeting to change the rules — either by adding a "Publisher" category (probably not a good idea) or else a motion to change the wording of 2.08 from ". . . shall not . . ." to ". . . need not be voted on by the Society membership." What's done is done, I suppose, but I do hope that future conventions follow the rules as they are written or else change them at the regular business meetings. The points I make are these: the Special Award is a *non*-competitive award given by the convention committee to whomever they think best deserves it, and no repeat *no* other awards may properly bear the name "Hugo" nor use the rocketship design until or unless the membership of the Society adds another category to the rules.

There are, after all, few enough restrictions on the convention committee in these rules — can not the committee keep to these few?

2.10 No Award: At the discretion of the individual convention committee, if a lack of votes in a specific category shows a marked lack of interest in that category on the part of the voters, the award in that category shall be canceled for that year.

2.11 Nominations and Voting: Selection of nominees for the final award voting shall be made by a poll conducted by the convention committee under rules determined by the convention committee.

Now, this 2.11 has an interesting history. At Seacon, the Hugo committee came up with recommendations for a nomination procedure. After the smoke of parliamentary maneuvers had cleared, it turned out that the effect of some amendment had been to strike out *all* provisions for the conduct of the nomination poll, therefore leaving the matter entirely in the hands of the convention committee. Chicon III accepted nominations from anyone who wrote; the Discon and Pacificon II accepted nominations only from members of the then current or just-previous convention. The principal difficulty is, really that who gets *nominated* depends on a very small number of voters (86 at Discon; 164 at Pacificon II), and consequently an exceedingly small number of voters acting together can put up their own candidate. In fact, Discon saw no evidence of this; apparently Pacificon II didn't either. (Dick Lupoff's campaign for "Savage Pellucidar" apparently brought about no more than a normal number of Burroughsfan votes for the thing.) How*ever*, at the Pacificon II business meeting, Harlan Ellison rose to tell a tale of woe:

According to Ellison, some-or-other pro author was expecting to win a Hugo, and, having won a Hugo, to get a profitable c*o*n*t*r*a*c*t for the work. Instead, some other writer was elected by the clod faaaans — and Ellison's protagonist was left both Hugo-less and contract-less. Now this, explained Ellison, meant real M*O*N*E*Y, lots of it, and he didn't for a minute intend to leave matters in the hands of mere fans and convention committees. He wanted another committee formed — right away — whose function would be to receive suggestions from anyone who might be interested, to read all the suggested works (or, one assumes, look at them, in the case of artists) and to come up with a nomination slate. Another motion, to appoint a Study Committee to investigate the whole Hugo system and make a preliminary recommendation at the '66 convention, was passed. Harlan was not to be put off — he still demanded his committee be formed without waiting for the Study Committee. Amazingly, the Ellison committee motion passed. In theory the next couple of cons should, therefore, have their slate of nominees for the final vote prepared by a committee.

The upshot of *this*, as you might guess, was still another crack in the continuity of conventions. The Loncon simply scrapped the whole notion of a nominating committee without discussion, at least pending the report of the Study Committee which Dick Lupoff is chairing. Despite a spectacular explosion of dramatics from one of those concerned ["if he doesn't get a Hugo maybe they'll consider him for an Oscar," as an unimpressed witness commented] this summary move seems, if not to have killed the idea outright, at least put it in the freezer until the next convention.

Now, the rest of section 2.11:

Final Award voting shall be by mail, with ballots sent only to society members (as defined in paragraph 1.02 above). Final Ballots shall standardize the alternatives given in each category to no more than five. Assignment of nominees nominated in more than one category to their proper category, and determination of eligibility of

nominees, shall be determined by the convention committee. Each person shall vote only once in each category in the final ballot.

The choice of "not more than five" nominees in a category is open to argument; with that many — or more — the final voting may be so divided that it's a matter of very few votes that divide the winner from the rest. On the other hand, if the number of nominees were standardized at (say) three, the question of who should be nominated and who not becomes *quite* sticky. Otherwise, you will note, wide discretion is given to the convention committee.

2.12 Tallying: Counting of all votes shall be done by the convention committee, which is responsible for all matters concerning awards.

2.13 Award Eligibility: No member of the current convention committee, nor any publication closely connected with them, shall be eligible for an award.

This last section can be a source of unhappiness to the convention committee if one or more of *them* have amateur publications in the running. Discon, for example, had two members who had Hugo possibilities. However, the undesirability of having somebody win — however honestly and fairly — one of the Hugos at his own convention is too plain. It strikes me that if the Ellison nominating committee ever becomes a reality, it ought to be subject to a similar exclusion rule.

2.14 The Hugo award will continue to be standardized, as to the design of the rocket ship, on the model presently in use. The design of the base shall be determined from year to year by each convention committee.

Now, as to the con site selection:

3.01 The Society shall choose the location of the next convention at a business meeting held at an advertised time during each annual World Science Fiction Convention, presided over by the chairman of the then current convention committee; or by a person designated by that committee. The business meeting shall be conducted under *Robert's Rules of Order, Revised* and such other rules as the then current convention committee may publish in the Program Book.

The point that the meeting be advertised is just elementary fairness. As for *Robert's Rules of Order, Revised* (the "revised" means the most recent edition of that title), these rules contain sufficient provisions for doing business rapidly in the absence of dissent that it is unnecessary to indicate that the chairman may use short cuts where applicable. A side note: there is *no* substitute for a chairman who is familiar with these rules; the rules themselves have been tested and revised over almost a hundred years of use. They are quite effective and efficient *if* the presiding officer be familiar with them.

Recently a question has come up about voting for the site by mail. The Constitution and Bylaws make no mention of such a thing, so *Robert's Rules* therefore govern — and *Robert's Rules* simply say that voting by proxy or absentee votes is allowed only if specific provision *is* made in the organization's bylaws. *Robert's Rules* also give a darn good reason to disallow absentee votes: the whole point of a deliberative business session — free public debate and discussion — is lost if the voters are not present to hear the deliberations. Anyway, as the rules now stand, absentee votes are out.

3.02 In order to assure an equitable distribution of convention sites, the North American continent is divided into three geographical divisions as follows:
Western Division: New Mexico, Colorado,

Wyoming, Montana, Saskatchewan, and states and provinces west; and the state of Baja California.

Central Division: All of Mexico except Baja California, and all states and provinces between the Western Division and the Eastern Division listed below.

Eastern Division: Florida, Georgia, South Carolina, North Carolina, Virginia, West Virginia, Pennsylvania, New York, Quebec, and states and provinces east.

This is the same division as set up at the San Francisco convention, with the addition of the Canadian Provinces and Baja California, and with the assignment of North Carolina to the Eastern Division; unaccountably, it was "Central" before.

3.03 Convention sites shall be rotated among these divisions in the order: West, Central, East. The bids of locations to hold a convention shall only be considered and voted on if they lie within the geographical division whose turn it is; except that the rule of rotation may be set aside by a vote of three-fourths voting on the location of the next convention. In the event of such setting aside, rotation shall be resumed the next year. For example, if the order of rotation is A, B, C; and if it is A's turn but the convention is given to a location in C, then B, the division which was neither set aside nor awarded the convention, shall be eligible next.

Historically, the rotation plan arose out of the bad feeling that followed the decision to award the '53 Worldcon to Philadelphia rather than San Francisco. The Philly bid was, according to Bob Madle, something of a spur-of-the-moment thing — one of the bid's most enthusiastic supporters was Dave Kyle. The result was a convention that Philadelphia didn't entirely want, and the near destruction of the San Francisco group. The rotation plan, on the other hand, allows a potential group to plan well ahead — and it *is* usually necessary to make arrangements with hotels, at least on a tentative basis, about two years in advance. Also, it allows a group to bid with a fair expectation of what the competition will be and what their chances are — and I think this goes a long way to helping a potential con committee keep from burning themselves out in the campaign before their con even begins. In 1962, when DC was bidding, the Philadelphia group could have made a bid, but they were willing to let us have it without a fight. Much the same situation existed in 1963 between Oakland and Los Angeles — there were two potential groups, but one didn't feel like making a fight of it.

Note well that the provisions above to cover an out-of-turn convention and the way the rotation is resumed do *not* apply to interruptions in the plan caused by an overseas con. In such a case:

3.04 Any location not on the North American continent may bid and may be selected at the business meeting of convention held on the North American continent. If the convention location is outside the North American continent, the rotation shall resume the following year, with locations in the Division replaced being then eligible to bid.

In other words, if it is the Central Division's turn, and London gets the con, then at London the Central Division locations are eligible again. Note also: if a con is held overseas, the next con following automatically returns to North America.

3.05 In the event the Society is without a properly selected location for the next annual convention, because of the resignation of the then current convention committee or other cause, the five most recent convention committee chairmen willing to serve shall be authorized to select the

next location for the World Science Fiction Convention.

This is a new bit — a provision to take care of an unforseen emergency which may leave the Society up in the air with no place to go. So far, no con committee has dissolved mid-flight, but it's a wonder that none has. As for the emergency crew, it was felt that a committee of past con-chairmen would hardly be likely to run off with the con site for themselves...

3.06 The date of the next convention and the dues to be charged for membership shall be proposed by each location bidding for that convention, prior to the selection of the next convention site. Such proposals are subject to modification by the business meeting.

Again, a new idea: instead of the date or the dues being matters for the Society to incorporate in its bylaws, they are left entirely up to the con committee, *except* that the bidding con committee must disclose its proposed date and dues in the course of making the bid. Thus, peculiar circumstances connected with a bid — for example, that August Bank Holiday, rather than Labor Day, is the date of the London convention — are taken care of without the necessity of making separate resolutions. And — if some con committee wants to put on a con with dues of $2 (or $4) — then that, along with all the other features of their bid, will be taken into account by the Society members when they vote on the next site.

4.01 Any change in the foregoing rules may take effect no sooner than the end of the convention during which such change is adopted.

In other words, the business meeting can change neither the rules for the Hugos to be presented at that convention nor can the meeting change the rules under which that meeting chooses the next con site. This is a simple precaution to insure that a bare majority will not first abolish the rotation plan and then vote in their out-of-turn favorite.

4.02 All previous by-laws, constitutions, and resolutions having the effect of by-laws and constitutions of the World Science Fiction Society are revoked.

That is, the tangled web of past rules is wiped away, and this codification takes effect instead.

Okay then, what about the matter of continuity? This divides into two parts: the convention committee, and the Society. Let's look at the con committee first.

Quite independently of the Society, the Chicon III committee incorporated the World Science Fiction Convention, Incorporated, under the laws of the State of Illinois. This corporation was a non-profit corporation, formed solely to cover the operations of the Chicon III con committee — to limit financial liability for one thing; to regularize the matter of income tax liability for another. The Discon committee operated under the same corporation; at the end of Chicon III and Discon, the outgoing committees transferred the corporation as described in the preceding chapter [9.02]. The Pacificon committee did not pass the corporate structure to London — the problems of foreign corporations doing business in England are too formidable — but will presumably pass the corporation to whoever has the convention in 1966.

The point to be remembered here is this: this corporation covers the con committee only; there is no continuing body of Elder Statesmen. In effect, each con committee is a separate entity — passing on the corporation is a simple stratagem to prevent each con committee from having to incorporate itself, a prohibitively expensive process in some states.

How about the Society? By implication, it *is* a continuing body, and these few rules, covering the Hugos and the way in which the site of the next con shall be chosen, *are* binding on each con committee. Note that this isn't much — all other matters are left wholly up to the convention committee, limited only by their own consciences and the State and Federal Criminal Statutes. The WSFS Inc. mess and the clutch of lawsuits that followed has convinced us that all con committees should be pretty much on their own.

But, on the other hand, when a con committee puts in a bid at a business meeting which is held under these rules, that potential con committee is saying in effect "We plan to put on a convention under the constitution and bylaws of the World Science Fiction Society, and we will follow these rules as best we can." It isn't an explicit commitment; we do not demand that a bidder promise to follow the rules; yet the implication is very clearly there.

The World Science Fiction Society is a continuing body — one formed to keep on picking sites for cons, to continue the award of Hugos to the people who best deserve them, and to attend cons — and have fun at them. Let's keep it that way.

XI. SUMMARY

11.01: The *first* thing you *must* do: get a hotel which has enough meeting space, enough bedrooms, reasonable prices, and a management that's interested in having you. If you don't have these in your town, forget it. If you do, you've got your biggest problem solved.

11.02: Set up a program, but don't try to stuff too much into the time available. For a big, high pressure con, consider a Friday thru Monday con. For a small con with few speakers available, consider doing practically nothing on Monday.

11.03: Keep track of what you've spent and what you expect to spend; what you've received and expect to receive; and consult the balance before spending for anything new. When in doubt, don't spend. With the $3 membership fee (I'm talking about North American cons, now) you can expect to break comfortably ahead of even. With a $2 fee, you'd sweat blood.

11.04: Don't depend on the auction to balance your

books. It can be a comfortable source of extra money, for — as an example — a set of *Proceedings.* And don't try to sell too many items in the time available.

11.05: If you want *Proceedings,* ask every speaker who normally works from a written speech for his manuscript, and ask beforehand. Even if he just works from notes, try to get them; they'll at least help in spelling hard words.

11.06: If the price of the banquet is too high, too few people will come. Unfortunately, there are no really cheap banquets available. As a *last* resort, you can do without a banquet.

11.07: Arrange things so that the costumes at the costume ball can be seen and announced; many costumes depend for their effectiveness on having their names announced. A band isn't necessary, but it helps, especially if they're set to play appropriate fanfares for the various costumes.

11.08: Publish a good set of progress reports and program book — don't be ashamed to put out a good, legible job of mimeography if you can't afford offset printing — but don't work yourself to death over the program book before the con begins.

11.09: If the auction material includes junk, separate out the junk and store, give, or throw it away. Program time is too valuable to waste on trying to sell an item worth one cent or two.

11.10: And, finally: if each member of the con committee feels the other members of the committee are working harder than he, and that he ought to do a bit more to catch up with his share, then you've got a successful committee working on a sure-to-be-successful con.

APPENDIX: TWO MORE FACETS

OF A PEARL OF GREAT PRICE

Howard DeVore: Coping with Crises

I never got to tell Eney some of the things that happened to me; I might as well recount them here.

First, the next time you hold a con try to arrange to have the tables in the room before the con opens. Such an agreement will prevent my being nabbed by the hotel while busy stealing tables from back in the storage area. As usual, this was solved by the old Dollar Bill Method.

There was also a little problem in getting unloaded. Roger Sims, Gregg Trend, and I started out in one car, following Broderick and Prophet in another car. We'd had breakfast with Marion Mallinger and Dirce Archer in Pittsburgh; I'd finished up the trip with them.

About 4:30 I'm in front of the hotel. Fred & Jim had dumped their load of my stock in Roger's car. I was watching Marion's car and driving Roger's car. I tried to locate a bell boy or the freight elevator. Finally I gave up, left the car parked in the loading area of the hotel, and walked around the hotel till I found the freight elevator . . . including the big sign, **CLOSED AFTER 3 PM**.

A conference with the bell captain brought the information that the elevator was closed and all the bell boys were busy, but if I'd wait in front of the hotel he would send one out soon to unload my boxes and carry them up to the second floor.

I had visions of the bell boy carrying sixty or seventy boxes upstairs at two bits a head. I walked back outside, got in the car, and parked it across the sidewalk in front of the freight elevator, then went back inside the hotel. In a few moments a bell boy passed me carrying a suitcase. I held a dollar bill in my hand and said: "Can you meet me back here in a few minutes?"

He made the round trip in less than five minutes. I held the bill out again and said, "I've got a carload of stuff outside and I'm in a hurry. If you can unlock that freight elevator, this is yours." He unlocked the door and I started stacking boxes. Twenty minutes later I had everything up in the display room!

You mentioned the rescue operation, so I'll fill in the details on that too. It started out rather slowly. I was visiting the N3F room, somewhere after midnight, and the room-phone rang. A voice said that some great big guy, with a convention badge, was passed out on the fourteenth floor and we should come get him. Janie Lamb had answered the phone; it sounded like a gag so she asked where the phoning fan was located. He was on the twelfth floor. Janie promised that we'd send someone up to check . . . and if it was a gag we'd also check out the room where the phone call originated, and bring a house dick with us.

The voice had reported that the man was too big to move. Janie told me that it sounded like Fred Prophet; remembering the way Fred had been putting it away an hour earlier convinced me that if anyone was passed out it probably *was* Fred. I recruited a half dozen fans and away we went. There was no body on the floor in the fourteenth floor corridor; obviously, it was a gag.

I decided that such practices should be discouraged and on the way back down I stepped off the elevator at the twelfth floor. I was going to read the riot act to someone, until I stumbled over a body . . . oh, so that's where you were! The fan phoning had simply quoted the wrong floor. I took one look at him — it was a man mountain of a Canadian — and decided I'd never move *this* one by myself! I shook him enough for him to mumble some words. Seems he didn't have a room:

"I sip inna N-three-F room."

Apparently drink had mellowed me; instead of doing the obvious I went back to the N3F room and recruited Ken Kruger and another fan. The three of us managed to get him to the room and hung his head over the side of the bed. later, someone went through his pockets, found the room key, and transferred him to his own room.

These Kreugers are handy people to have around!

Bob Pavlat: Casual Reflections on Con Committees

Some unlucky night in the future someone in the audience may catch me commenting on how easy it is to put on a convention. Ignore me. I don't know what I'm talking about. I don't to this day know what goes into putting on a convention. For me, it required less work than, say, an issue of *Fanzine Index*. I think EES (Evans, Eney and Scithers) correctly gauged the amount of work they thought they might be able to get out of me, and gave me that much and no more. It wasn't work.

I've heard Scithers, Evans, and Eney say they didn't work either. I don't believe them. I know that Evans received and processed a tremendous amount of mail, requiring almost daily posting of books, replies to enquiries, mailout of material, and the like. Eney received Art Show materials [and sent them back afterward], mocked up and set up progress reports and the program book and did a lot of the printing. Scithers oversaw everything, set up the program items, made all masquerade ball arrangements including the band and special effects, corresponded with everyone under the sun, took care of Hugo bases and plates, did the printing with Eney's assistance, and too much else to remember. From my lofty diplomatic post I called the hotel and convention bureau a few times, wrote a couple of dozen letters, helped folding programs and progress reports and stuffing envelopes, but certainly none of it was any strain.

I can't directly comment on the success of the Discon. I saw about 15 minutes of the auction, heard Evans's introduction of Seabury Quinn, and was present during the banquet and the business session. The rest of the time I was at the registration desk, or catching up on eating, or chasing down some member of the hotel staff (not that there was trouble, but there are always minor items like how about some more chairs, where the heck is the registration desk's telephone, and we've sold 300 banquet tickets and is it all right to go on or do you want to establish a cut-off time), or moving stuff to and from the room to the convention area. There *is* a lot to be done during the convention proper. Most of it seemed to me to go smoothly. We committed a few minor goofs by failing to anticipate certain things, but I think most of them went unnoticed. From these indications, from a few personal comments, and from a few notes in the fan press, the Discon was apparently at least a good convention.

There were three things the con committee wanted to do, which we talked over and agreed upon before the Chicago bid. First priority was to run on a budget, and not spend money until we could pinpoint exactly where the money would come from. This was never a problem — we were in the black before we returned to D.C. from Chicago, and remained in the black throughout. The second was to run a fairly relaxed convention. This was achieved reasonably well, although despite George's attempts to keep the program relaxed there were still items vying for time. The third thing was a hope that we could prove that running a convention was not a man-killing job. We knew that some had claimed it was such a job, we knew fans previously involved with committees who wanted no further part of any future ones, and we knew of shattered friendships.

You seldom find workhorses like EES; that's possibly part of the reason nobody felt himself to be under any great con strain. We had almost no disagreement on the committee, and this of course helped. Our internal capability to print the booklets possibly helped some, as did the foresight of getting the Hugo Awards well in advance of the con (these were picked up at the 1962 MidWestCon). There was no financial strain, the hotel was beautifully cooperative, and there were many members of the club (and people outside the Washington area) who were willing to lend a hand.

The heavy work occurred in the last couple of weeks before the con, and resulted primarily from the printing of the Program Book. This is a sizeable operation. It's as big a job as it is primarily because of the number of ads carried. I'm not sure if the ads are worth the effort. They probably are, if the money is needed. Scithers showed some sign of strain here (he was the man doing most of the work) but prior to the con this was the only sign of overwork on any one of the committee. The first day-and-a-half of the con were hectic — would the hotel come through, has so-and-so arrived yet, we need more nickels for change and all the banks are closed, this is the last box of card-holders . . . Finally, though, it's banquet time, you can forget about the registration desk from here on out, no more banquet sales to fret about, the food is reasonably good for a banquet, and the master of ceremonies takes over.

I've seen a lot of advice given on how to run a convention. The advice that I was given most frequently was, "Don't get involved!" I helped some, and it was fun. From the Discon, I'm convinced that there are some things that are needed to put on a convention. You need a head man with good common sense and a sense of showmanship. You need a couple of reliable workers, as treasurer and editor. And you need from three to ten people, quite possibly teenagers, who can handle a job without too much supervision. One more qualification for the head man — he must know how to delegate, and have the knowledge of people required to delegate to the right man. Your three primary people must in general be able to get along together. If any group can meet these qualifications, then there's no good reason that they should be hesitant about putting on a convention. One thing the Washington committee did lack was the feminine point of view. There were no women on the committee, and all four of us were bachelors. Peggy Rae McKnight helped lend the feminine touch in the last moments of preparation and during the con; advice like hers adds a little here and there.

A couple of people, former con members, have said it would be perfectly feasible and possible to put on a con in Las Vegas even if they lived in, let's say, Atlanta. I think they are right. There is a minimum essential amount of work. It only becomes a back breaker if you want to do more than enough.

THE END

www.ingramcontent.com/pod-product-compliance
Lightning Source LLC
Chambersburg PA
CBHW031215270326
41931CB00006B/572